# HOW TO

# STUDY

# EFFECTIVELY

BY

JIM CORONEOS, B. Sc. Dip. Ed.

AND

JOHN SMITH, B. Sc. Dip. Ed.

This book is available from any recognised bookseller or contact:

Business Address

Jim Coroneos
(Rear) 580 Old South Head Rd
Rose Bay, N.S.W. 2029
Australia

Telephone: All hours (02) 9371 8530
Fax: All hours (02) 9371 7099

Postal Address

Jim Coroneos
P.O.Box 25
Rose Bay N.S.W. 2029
Australia

Printed and bound in Australia by
McPherson's Printing Group

# CONTENTS

# CONTENTS

# PREFACE

**A)** WHAT THIS BOOK IS ABOUT.

1) This book is a collection of directives to aid in the study of all subjects. These directives have been seen to work in ALL students over many years.

2) You will be shown how to develop your powers of memory and concentration.

3) You will be given step by step instructions on how to organise your work.

4) If you follow these directives, you will be guaranteed improvement.

**B)** WHAT THIS BOOK IS NOT ABOUT

1) This book is NOT a 'study guide' containing what you need to know for a particular exam. Study guides serve a totally different purpose.

2) This book is not a summary or all the facts you need to know.

3) Nor is it a tutorial book, explaining the 'hard' parts of the course. So do not look for hundreds of worked examples, lists of formulae or tests of achievement - they won't appear.

4) What is promised is that if you apply these techniques your marks will improve, your ability in all subjects will rise, and your self-confidence will increase.

**C)** WHO THIS BOOK IS FOR

1) This book is for students who are tired of failing tests.

2) It is for students who wish to improve their overall results.

3) It is for students who, while achieving well in school, do so only by long hard hours of slogging.

4) It is for students who can pass a test on topic A but have forgotten the results of topic A a month later and hence fail topic B.

5) It is for students who can pass monthly tests, but fail the yearly exam.

6) It is for students who cannot find the work they did a month ago.

7) It is for students whose idea of study is gained from newspaper articles, TV programmes or peer folklore.

8) It is for students who feel that the amount of work expected of them is too great.

9) It is for students who can feel themselves falling behind in their work.

10) It is for students just starting school.

11)    It is for students about to sit for college or university entrance
       exams.

12)    It is for tertiary students who find that what lecturers do is totally
       different from what teachers do.

13)    It is for private study students - that unseen army of students who have
       no contact with other students or teachers.

14)    It is for parents who have watched in despair as their comprehension of
       what their offspring is studying has plummetted.

15)    And last, it is for teachers, those to whom students seldom come for
       advice and who, since they were always good at their subject, cannot
       understand why everyone is not as good as they are.

## D)  WHY BUY THIS BOOK

1)     Each year, just before the college/university entrance exams are set,
       newspapers across the country get the services of 'experts' to write
       guidelines on how to study.  These are published with great fanfare
       about a MONTH before the exams!!  Each year, thousands of students are
       told that if only they will 'organise' themselves, if only they will
       do thousands of examples, write hundreds of essays, if only this and if
       only that, they will - presumably - live happily ever after.

       I imagine a lot of newspapers are sold - but I don't for a moment think
       that grades are improved by advice such as this - however well-
       intentioned.

2)     Imagine yourself the night before your exam - be it an important final
       or a class test :

       You have your handy newspaper guide, your textbooks, paper and pen, all
       ready to start :

       a)     First you must 'organise' yourself - but how?

       Quickly summarise the entire course?  List every formula?  Write out
       worked examples from the textbook?  Read the entire play or novel?  Or
       what?

       b)     Taking mathematics as an example, you must do thousands - well
       hundreds - of examples.  Let's see .... it's 7 p.m. now, the exam's at
       9 a.m. tomorrow, that's 14 hours if you don't sleep - say 5 minutes per
       example, that's 12 examples per hour, 168 examples that you can do!

       *Not the best advice is it?*

       However year after year, the same advice sells more newspapers, and
       really **that** is what it is intended to do - NOT help the student.

       AND EVEN IF YOU START 3 MONTHS BEFORE THE EXAM - for a large exam that's
       more than average - what does it mean 'do hundreds of examples'?

       Which examples?  The ones you did in class? - Why?  The ones you didn't
       do in class? - How?

In either case you're probably wasting time - in the first case, if you've already done them, why do them again?  In the second case, they were probably not set as class work because they cover work that is too hard or is not in your course.

c)    But more to the point - have you ever tried to sit down and 'do maths'?  Odds are that the first example you try will stop you.  So you try the next.  Maybe you get it out.  Great!!  But then things go bad.  You get a couple more wrong.  Then you can't understand the question.  Now the self-doubt starts.  You're sure that everyone else can do it - after all they're smart.  Maybe if you'd paid more attention in class.  But nobody really understood it in class anyway.  What do you expect with such a lousy teacher ....

And so on.

3)   Perhaps you should turn to the ever-popular 'study guides'.  After all everyone else uses them - why shouldn't you?

Study guides are available at any bookstore or newsagency.  They are not expensive and claim to be able to tell you everything you need to know on virtually any subject.  They are usually divided into topics, worked examples or trial essays are given to 'explain' the important parts, and then on the next topic.  There are three problems with them :

a)    Say the topic is Trigonometry.  Definitions are given - then the worked examples.  But in order to read the worked example, it may be necessary for you to be able to solve equations, and this you could never do.  Hence the worked example is useless to you.

b)    When the worked example is chosen for you, how can you expect it to help you with the problems that YOU have?  As you will see, the underlying theme of <u>this</u> book is that you and your problems are unique.  Therefore how can one worked example - or ten - help EVERYONE?

c)    Because study guides cover the entire course, because every topic has numerous worked examples or sample essays, because they are used by so many people, because they are nicely typed and bound, the student (you!) is tempted to believe that the study guide is GOOD and that if the student (you!!) cannot understand it or if the student's problems (yours) aren't answered, then it is the student's (your) FAULT.  Before long the student ends up thinking that he or she is stupid!!  This of course may be true, but because your questions are not answered by a study guide is no proof of it.

4)   Whichever path you choose to follow, remember that self-doubt and self-destruction have to be taught to you.  <u>They are NOT natural states of mind</u>.

As the saying goes :

*"YOU ARE ALL YOU'VE GOT - SO YOU'D BETTER MAKE THE MOST OF IT."*

E)   HOW THIS BOOK IS SET OUT

Because this book is aimed at many groups of people, I have split it up under the following headings :

# PREFACE

While you may fit into just one category - to get the most out of the book you should READ IT ALL. As you will see, the book is based on the premise that we are all different and hence, while you may be still in school, the section on teachers, say, may contain an idea that you can use to your own advantage.

F) REASONS FOR STUDY OVER AND ABOVE SET HOMEWORK

i) The overriding reasons for study time is that *EFFECTIVE STUDY WILL MAKE YOUR SCHOOL-LIFE EASIER AND MORE INTERESTING.*

You will begin to perceive that subjects that you found incomprehensible and therefore boring, do in fact make sense.

You will find that you develop more interests in life as you understand more and can see how different ideas fit together.

ii) By learning how to study, you will *IMPROVE YOUR CAREER PROSPECTS.* The sacrifices you make now, will reap their reward later.

Studying is a highly artificial way of spending time. It is also very hard work. While there is no technique which can make hard work easy, *IT IS CERTAINLY POSSIBLE TO MAKE SURE THAT HARD WORK IS ALSO EFFECTIVE WORK.*

iii) *EFFECTIVE STUDY NOW WILL ENSURE SUCCESS IN EXAMINATION.* While exams are not the only reason for study, it is a fact of life that many institutions hold the performance in them as a necessary entrance requirement.

iv) *EFFECTIVE STUDY TECHNIQUES GIVE THE STUDENT TOOLS TO USE IN ANY FUTURE LEARNING SITUATION, BE IT BUSINESS, TRADE SCHOOL OR UNIVERSITY.*

# CHAPTER ONE

## GENERAL PRINCIPLES OF EFFECTIVE STUDY

### SUMMARY

1....EFFECTIVE STUDY HELPS CONSOLIDATE THE DAY'S WORK

2....EFFECTIVE STUDY HELPS PLACE NEW KNOWLEDGE IN PERSPECTIVE

3....EFFECTIVE STUDY FORCES YOU TO MAKE CONNECTIONS BETWEEN
       KNOWLEDGE AREAS

4....EFFECTIVE STUDY WILL MAKE LIFE EASIER AND MORE INTERESTING BOTH
       AT SCHOOL AND LATER

Before we start, a very important point must be made :

STUDY IS NOT HOMEWORK

The following discussion is not intended to apply to homework - only to the study which is over and above the homework.  As you will discover, if you apply the principles of this book, your study will MINIMISE the time needed for homework, and your homework will MINIMISE the time needed for study.  That, however, is a bonus and you should not confuse the two.

Believe it or not, many students do not think that study helps at all!  Unfortunately they are too often quite correct - but that's not because study itself is useless, but because their method of study is NOT EFFECTIVE.

But to start with, let's review a few reasons for the use of EFFECTIVE study.

1)    EFFECTIVE STUDY WILL HELP YOU CONSOLIDATE THE DAY'S WORK

How many times has it happened to you, that while cramming for an exam, you come across an idea that you remember covering in class, but which now escapes you altogether?

This happens to us all the time.  Our minds can remember just so much, and unless we put an effort into remembering something - be it a date in history or the name of the person next door - we will forget it.

THIS CANNOT BE STRESSED TOO MUCH :  UNLESS WE CONSOLIDATE AND REINFORCE OUR KNOWLEDGE, IT WILL BE LOST - THIS IS A MAJOR REASON FOR HOME STUDY.

And be sure you believe it!  You will read in the afternoon newspapers, you will see on television, you will hear from friends that we remember everything.  They will tell you that each item of information is etched indelibly into your brain cells and can never be erased.  That may be true.

But you can NEVER remember everything when you need it.  It may come to you on your death bed as your life flashes before your eyes, *but it won't come to you tomorrow in the exam.*

2)    STUDY OVER AND ABOVE WRITTEN HOMEWORK, WILL ALLOW YOU TO PLACE THE DAY'S KNOWLEDGE IN PERSPECTIVE.

For example, you may learn in a science class that 'hot air rises'. Ten days later, you learn in a geography class that the higher you are above sea-level the colder it gets. Clearly this contradicts what you learned in science. But most people have never noticed the contradiction!! They have not got their knowledge in perspective.

Obviously there must be a way out of the contradiction, but unless your knowledge is filed away correctly and brought out to be re-examined regularly you will find yourself getting B's where you used to get A's. (Since this book aims to help you STUDY EFFECTIVELY, do not look for answers to contradictions. That is what textbooks and teachers are for.)

3)    EFFECTIVE STUDY, AS THE PRECEDING EXAMPLE SHOWS, ALLOWS - OR RATHER FORCES YOU TO MAKE CONNECTIONS BETWEEN YOUR KNOWLEDGE AREAS.

Each area will then support others, making recall easier. (This is covered in more detail later.)

4)    EFFECTIVE STUDY WILL MAKE LIFE EASIER AND MORE INTERESTING AT SCHOOL.

But you will not always be at school! Sooner or later you will make the transition to the working world, where it will be assumed that, if nothing else, you have learned how to learn. No-one who works can afford not to continually upgrade their knowledge. The world changes too quickly for that. *So learning how to study EFFECTIVELY now, will serve you throughout life.*

## CHAPTER TWO

## HOW TO DEVELOP GOOD HABITS AND PREPARE A STUDY TIMETABLE

SUMMARY

1....A LITTLE STUDY EACH DAY MAKES LIFE EASIER

2....PARENTS MAY HELP

3....DEVELOP YOUR OWN PERSONAL TIMETABLE

4....SEPARATE SIMILAR SUBJECTS ON YOUR TIMETABLE

5....MAKE YOUR TIMETABLE AS PRECISE AS POSSIBLE

6....KEEP A BALANCE BETWEEN SUBJECTS

7....STUDY THE 'HARDEST' SUBJECTS FIRST

8....NOT ALL SUBJECTS REQUIRE THE SAME AMOUNT OF TIME

9....THERE IS NO ONE TIMETABLE FOR ALL STUDENTS

10...PLAN YOUR LEISURE TIME AND TIMETABLE IT

11...USE SHORT PERIODS OF TIME TO ADVANTAGE

12...USE TRAVEL TIME TO REVISE

13...A GOOD NIGHT'S WORK CONSISTS OF ...

14...DON'T DESPAIR - BE KIND TO YOURSELF

15...SAMPLE TIMETABLES

You probably can't remember learning how to clean your teeth, but if you have a younger brother or sister to watch, you will see a strange sight :

What is the simplest of tasks for you is a major problem for them.  They can't get the top off the paste, they don't know what to do with the brush while they get the paste, the paste falls on the floor and so on.  Obviously, it can only be the fact that we have done it so often that makes it easy.

So too with study.

1)     IF YOU RESOLVE TO DO A LITTLE EACH DAY, YOU WILL FIND THAT IT BECOMES EASIER.

       What to do with the time you set aside for study, we'll cover later.  But a determination to do something each day is your first step.

2)     AND IF IT MEANS THAT YOU MUST GET SOMEONE TO SUPERVISE YOUR WORK, THEN DO SO.

       Your parents are the obvious choice if you are still at school.  They can help, for example, by ensuring that things are quiet around the house during your study period.

3)  **HENCE YOU SHOULD TRY TO FOLLOW A TIMETABLE.**

This will ensure that you allocate your study time evenly rather than spending all your time on your favourite subject. The timetable will rule your life for the duration of the course, so you should spend some thought on its construction.

4)  **YOU SHOULD SEPARATE SIMILAR SUBJECTS, OR 'MEMORY' SUBJECTS ON YOUR TIMETABLE.**

For example, you would not study History, then English, then Geography. A better split of subjects would be : English, then Mathematics, then History. Similarly you would not study Mathematics then Physics, but would put Geography between them.

5)  **MAKE YOUR TIMETABLE AS PRECISE AS POSSIBLE.**

Thus if you know that you will need to revise Topics A and B before a class test then write them into your timetable. And after the test take them out again. This means that your timetable must be CONSTANTLY REVISED and UPDATED.

6)  **REMEMBER TO KEEP THE BALANCE BETWEEN SUBJECTS.**

Subject A may be more interesting to you than any other, but the others must also be studied. If you put off studying them, you will build up panic in yourself which will make studying them well-nigh impossible.

You may like to keep a record of what you have studied in a diary, and compare it with what you intended to study, over, say, the period of a week. This will allow you to make any adjustments in the quantity and distribution of your time during the following week.

7)  **PLAN TO STUDY THE 'HARDEST' SUBJECTS WHEN YOU ARE ALERT.**

Some persons function best in the hour before breakfast. Some are night-owls. You know the best time for you. Use that time to tackle the subjects you find most difficult. Soon you will find that your 'hardest' subjects are becoming easier - so revise your timetable again.

8)  **DON'T THINK THAT ALL SUBJECTS REQUIRE THE SAME AMOUNT OF TIME.**

You will find that it is IMPOSSIBLE to spend the same time on each anyway. By experiment you may find that spending more than 15 minutes on French is wasted time. So don't. It will mean that French has to occur more often on your timetable, but bear in mind that, for you, two lots of 15 minutes may be much better than one lot of 30 minutes. Remember that it is EFFECTIVE study that counts, not the amount of time spent at your desk.

9)  **DON'T EVER THINK THAT THERE IS ONE TIMETABLE FOR EVERYONE.**

Your friend's timetable will be of NO USE to you, even though you do the same subjects, sit together in class and so on. EFFECTIVE STUDY IS A TOTALLY PERSONAL THING.

**10)** PLAN YOUR LEISURE TIME AND PUT IT ON THE TIMETABLE.

Too many students forget that their mind needs a rest, a regular rest, and that their body needs exercise. Physical fitness will make your ability to study, learn and recall just that much easier.

**11)** USE SHORT PERIODS OF TIME TO ADVANTAGE.

Too often we have 15 minutes to spend waiting for a bus, or for dinner to be served, and we waste it. If you practise using every short period of time to revise something or start a problem in mathematics or write the plan of an essay, you will find that these short periods of time become very valuable to you.

**12)** USE TRAVEL TIME TO REVISE

Many students, both city and country, spend a lot of time travelling to school. This time is usually spent with friends, talking over the previous night's television. You can, of course, spend it more fruitfully by revising previous work, planning the day's work and so on. If you are lucky enough to find another student who is doing the same course as yourself, you can arrange to discuss topics of your work, to exchange ideas and so on. You can achieve much productive work in this way, leaving more time free after school.

**13)** A GOOD NIGHT'S WORK SHOULD CONSIST OF THREE PARTS :

*1.   SET HOMEWORK AND PREPARATION FOR THE NEXT DAY'S WORK.*

*2.   REVISION OF THE DAY'S WORK WITH UPDATING OF SUMMARIES.*

*3.   STUDY AS SET OUT IN THE TIMETABLE.*

If, as well, you can include twenty minutes exercise, you will be able to work at optimum level.

**14)** DON'T DESPAIR.

The first time normal human beings try to put a timetable on their lives, they get feelings of depression : their lives are no longer their own, the spontaneity has gone from their lives and so on. When this happens to you, remember the story of the toothpaste - I have never met a person who gave up eating because he or she couldn't bear to brush his or her teeth afterwards. Unfortunately, you need to clean your teeth if you would like to keep them and you need to study to achieve the goals you have set yourself. You don't have to clean your teeth and you don't have to study, but the results are similar.

**15)** SAMPLE TIMETABLES.

Obviously you will need to develop your own timetable. To give you some idea of how these MAY look, you will find sample timetables in the Glossary at the end of the book.

# CHAPTER THREE

## ENVIRONMENT - WHERE TO STUDY

SUMMARY

1....STUDYING WITH BACKGROUND NOISE

2....FREE YOURSELF FROM INTERRUPTIONS

3....FRESH AIR VERSUS STUDYING AT THE BEACH

4....HAVE A SPECIAL PLACE TO STUDY

5....STUDYING IN BED IS A WASTE OF TIME

6....ATTEND TO YOUR GENERAL HEALTH

Again these topics are necessary to mention here but will probably be known to you already.

By environment I mean the physical place or places you set aside for study. And again there is no best place - different environments suit different people. And because of this, I must mention a few general comments to overcome the nonsense you will hear from well-meaning relatives and friends.

It is not true that people need absolute quiet in order to study. *But it does not follow that you need to have a radio blaring.* And while short breaks are a good idea, *it does not follow that answering the telephone every ten minutes will aid your study.* And while you should be reasonably comfortable, *it does not follow that all study should be done in bed.*

1)  QUIET IS THE BEST.

    I know that this point can be argued. It has been found that very quiet background music has no measurable effect on concentration. But as soon as the announcer comes on, or a commercial break occurs, ability to study falls away. Make your own decision.

2)  FREE YOUR ENVIRONMENT FROM INTERRUPTIONS.

    Interrruptions, be they telephone calls, radio commercials or whatever, will lower your concentration. With friends, you can tell them when you will be free to talk and they won't mind. On the other hand, bear in mind that talking to a friend ABOUT THE WORK YOU ARE DOING, will benefit both of you. Again make your decision.

3)  FRESH AIR IS NEEDED FOR YOUR MIND TO WORK AT ITS BEST.

    Ensure that you have fresh air around you. Since a lot of your time studying will be done in winter, the temptation is to turn the heater on. This may make you sleepy or sap your vitality. In summer, you may be tempted to take your work outside in the sun. Again you may become drowsy but more than likely you will be disturbed. Either way you lose.

4)    HAVE A SPECIAL PLACE TO STUDY.

If you can have such a place, you will find that it is easier to commence work and to concentrate on your work, than if you study in the lounge room on one night, the kitchen the next and so on.

In your special study place, you should have pens, pencils, paper, books, calculators and all equipment that you will need throughout the night. Breaking off to search for a pencil-sharpener will harm your concentration.

The lighting is important. Overhead lights are not designed to read by. You should have a reading lamp shining at an angle to the page you are reading (so that you escape the glare.)

5)    STUDYING IN BED IS A WASTE OF TIME.

Use your bed for rest, your desk for study. You spend so much time in bed that your subconscious mind will start relaxing you ready for sleep as soon as you lie down. You cannot combine study and relaxation without spoiling both.

6)    ATTEND TO YOUR GENERAL HEALTH.

You should pay particular attention to your diet, your sleep, your exercise and your recreation. Too many students fail to do this only to find that they fall ill the day before the exam.

Remember too that recreation does not mean sleep. Sometimes a total break from work may be the best medicine. A weekend spent bushwalking will refresh you as no amount of sleep ever could. You return to your work a new person, your ability to concentrate, and to absorb new ideas heightened.

# CHAPTER FOUR

# HOW TO CONCENTRATE

## SUMMARY

1....WHAT IS CONCENTRATION

2....THE 'SECRET' OF CONCENTRATION

3....THE 'SERIES OF QUESTIONS/ACTIVITIES' APPROACH

4....CONCENTRATION IS AN ACTIVITY

5....FIND REASONS TO BE INTERESTED IN THE SUBJECT

6....TAKE SHORT BREAKS

7....SET TIME LIMITS

8....HOW TO START THE NIGHT

1)   WHAT IS CONCENTRATION EXACTLY?

There are two experiments that you can perform right now to introduce the topic of concentration:

EXPERIMENT ONE :  *If you relax as much as possible, and stare at any point on the page, very quickly you will find that, even though you are 'concentrating' on the spot on the page, you have drifted into some dream world.*

EXPERIMENT TWO :  *The second is a yoga exercise and you really need a yoga teacher to lead you through it, for the first time.  Close your eyes and think of a flower.  Note its colour, its fragrance, its feel.  Notice how the colour and the feel go together.  In your mind turn the flower over and see the stem.  See how the stem joins onto the flower, both supporting and complementing it.*

A good teacher can continue this patter for a very long time and it is very easy for you to concentrate on the imaginary flower - and nothing else - throughout.

IN EACH EXPERIMENT you 'concentrated' but the effects in each case are totally different.  For effective studying we need to be able to study our work as we studied the flower.

But does this mean that we need a yoga teacher on call?  Not at all.  The point of the yoga exercise is to show us that the teacher is irrelevant.  For what did the teacher do that we could not do ourselves?  The teacher asked questions - so can we; the teacher suggested we view the flower from all angles - so could we; the teacher asked us to compare the properties of the flower with each other - we could have done that just as easily.  In fact, the teacher got us to concentrate by continually asking us to DO SOMETHING with the flower!!

2)   **THE SECRET OF CONCENTRATION IS TO GET YOUR MIND TO DO SOMETHING WITH THE THING WE ARE STUDYING**

If we let the mind do as it pleases, it will wander.  However, if we continually bring it back to the idea that we are trying to master, if we get it to pick up the idea and turn it around, if we see how the various parts of the idea fit together, if we count the number of parts in the idea and so on, we will learn the idea.  If we further see how the idea fits into our world, what other ideas depend on it, what it depends on, what changes it has brought and so on, we will also be able to USE the idea - which is what we should be aiming to do.

3)   **THE SERIES OF QUESTIONS/ACTIVITIES APPROACH.**

As a practical step therefore, you should try to get a series of questions or activities together that suit your subject (they will be different for each subject.)

For instance, you may be trying to study a passage of history.  You could therefore :

i)     *Ask yourself WHAT is going on.*

ii)    *Ask yourself HOW it could have happened.*

iii)   *Ask yourself WHO was responsible.*

iv)    *Ask yourself WHERE it happened.*

v)     *Ask yourself WHEN it occurred.*

vi)    *Ask yourself WHY it happened.*

These questions force you to look more closely at the material you are reading.  Sentences that you would gloss over take on an extra meaning if you are looking for something.  The questions turn you from a PASSIVE reader into an ACTIVE one.

Or you may be trying to learn a proof in geometry.  You could force your mind to DO SOMETHING by using the following approach :

i)     *Read through the material quickly.*

ii)    *Read again mentally noting the main ideas.*

iii)   *Read again; writing down the main ideas.*

iv)    *Go over the notes you have made, seeing if the argument makes sense.*

v)     *Review the argument in your mind.*

vi)    *Jot down the argument from memory.*

vii)   *Read the material a last time to make sure you have missed nothing.*

As you get better at this technique you will certainly change it and adapt it to your own needs.  The moral is :

CONCENTRATION IS AN ACTIVITY

4)    CONCENTRATION IS AN ACTIVITY.

      *YOU CAN'T EXPECT YOUR MIND TO CONCENTRATE, YOU MUST CONSTANTLY GOAD IT
      INTO ACTION!*

      And you will be disappointed!!  The first few times you try this technique,
      you will find it works.  But as the novelty wears off, you will find that
      it is still difficult to concentrate on things that don't interest you.
      Don't despair, you are in good company.

5)    BUT WHAT YOU CAN DO, IS TO TRY TO FIND REASONS FOR BEING
      INTERESTED IN THE SUBJECT.

      SOMEone must find this topic interesting; find that person and ask him/her.

      Does this subject fit in with any other subjects; find the connection.

      With this subject/idea can I make money so that I don't have to work after
      school?  Think about it.

      Does this idea lead on to any other idea that I find interesting?

      Can I use this idea to win a prize in the 'Most Boring Idea Ever Thought Of'
      essay competition?

      If you try, you will find something interesting in just about any topic.
      And that will aid your concentration.

6)    TAKE SHORT BREAKS.

      Even under the best conditions you will not be able to keep concentration
      at a consistently high pitch.

      As you feel your concentration starting to fade, a short walk, a glass of
      water, even stretching exercises are all activities that will give your mind
      a short break.

      You will find that two half hour periods of concentration will make for more
      EFFECTIVE STUDY that one full hour.

7)    SET TIME LIMITS.

      If you have given yourself a half hour in which to solve a problem in
      physics, you will find that you will probably take exactly one half hour.
      But if you had given yourself 20 minutes, say, you may have found that you
      could have solved the same problem in the reduced time.

      Similarly, if you have an essay to write, set a time limit in which that
      essay MUST be written.

      This technique is used by some of the most successful people in all walks of
      life.  (It is a adaption of Parkinson's Law which states that *'Work expands
      to fill the time available for it'*.)

      Further to this idea, you may be trying to understand some piece of
      mathematics.  You try it once and can't understand it.  You try it again
      with the same result.  If you fail on the third try, put it aside and come
      back to it when your mind is fresh.

8)    HOW TO START THE NIGHT.

Many students can work well enough 'once they get started'. but getting started often seems an impossibility. To overcome this, you need GOOD HABITS in starting your work. You should try the following :

*i)*    SIT AT YOUR STUDY PLACE. RECALL EACH LESSON OF THE DAY AND IN 2 OR 3 MINUTES FOR EACH, JOT DOWN THE IMPORTANT ASPECTS THAT YOU REMEMBER.

*ii)*   OPEN YOUR BOOKS AND CHECK YOUR MEMORY, NOTING THOSE THINGS THAT YOU FAILED TO REMEMBER CORRECTLY.

*iii)*  NOW YOUR MIND IS TUNED IN TO WORK, YOU SHOULD START YOUR SET HOMEWORK AS PER YOUR TIMETABLE.

16

# CHAPTER FIVE

## HOW TO DEVELOP A GOOD MEMORY

SUMMARY

1....REMEMBERING IS AN ACTIVITY

2....ASSOCIATE YOUR NEW KNOWLEDGE WITH YOUR OLD

3....REGULAR BREAKS ALLOW THE MIND TO CONSOLIDATE

4....CRAMMING IN THE LAST FEW WEEKS IS COUNTERPRODUCTIVE

5....NOTE-TAKING IS CRUCIAL

6....USE KEY-WORDS

7....REMEMBERING LISTS OF KEY-WORDS

8....TRY TO GET AN OVERVIEW BEFORE LEARNING THE DETAILS

9....STUDY WITH A PEN IN YOUR HAND

10...STATE KEY POINTS ALOUD

11...EXPECT YOUR LEARNING TO SPEED UP AND SLOW DOWN

12...REST OR SLEEP AFTER YOU HAVE STUDIED

13...REVISE - REVISE - REVISE

14...DISCUSS YOUR WORK WITH FRIENDS

There are two distinct parts to having a good memory :

a)    getting the information in,

b)    getting it out.

There are several simple principles here.

1)    REMEMBERING IS AN ACTIVITY

As you saw in the concentration exercises, we can go about things actively or passively.  TO BE ACTIVE IN REMEMBERING SOMETHING, WE MUST USE ENERGY.

If you think when you hear a joke :  *"What a great joke, I'll never forget that one because it's so funny"*, then you can bet that you will forget the joke!!  The reason is simple :  you believed - like most people - that interest alone is sufficient to remember.  *This is not so!*

You must expend energy to remember.  *YOU MUST THINK ABOUT IT - NOT JUST THE WORDS, BUT THE MEANINGS UNDERNEATH THE WORDS.*  You must compare the joke with others of the same type, and contrast it with different types.

You can think of your memory as being made like an onion. Like the layers in the onion, there are layers in the memory. When you first read or hear a piece of information, it is stored in the outer layer of memory. By thinking about the piece of information you can get it stored at deeper and deeper layers of memory. When you come to get rid of useless knowledge, (i.e. to forget it), the first to go is the information stored in the outer layer. Hence the need to get the information into a deeper layer. *THE ENERGY YOU EXPEND NOW WILL BE REWARDED BY HAVING A STRONGER MEMORY LATER.*

2)    TRY TO TIE YOUR NEW KNOWLEDGE TO AS MANY OTHER AREAS OF KNOWLEDGE AS YOU CAN.

*IF YOU CAN FORM AS MANY AND VARIED ASSOCIATIONS BETWEEN THE NEW KNOWLEDGE AND THE KNOWLEDGE YOU ALREADY POSSESS, THEN ALL THE PIECES OF YOUR KNOWLEDGE ACT AS TRIGGERS FOR YOUR MEMORY RECALL.*

So, you may have learned in science that heat causes things to expand. You may already know from physical education class that you should never go into a sauna after exercise. Now, both pieces of knowledge involve HEAT - therefore maybe there is a connection. If you can find out what the connection is - by asking or reading - then the two pieces of information become one. And if you recall one it will automatically trigger the recall of the other.

There are obviously other benefits that come from finding connections between areas of knowledge, but here I am only concerned with how the association of ideas helps your memory.

3).    YOU SHOULD GIVE YOURSELF REGULAR BREAKS FROM STUDYING.

THIS ALLOWS YOUR MIND TO FORM ASSOCIATIONS BETWEEN THE NEW KNOWLEDGE AND THE OLD.

As you saw, more associations mean better recall later. It is as though the outer layers of the memory onion become soaked with information. If we do not give the information time to seep into the deeper levels of the onion, i.e. we keep on studying and putting more information into the outer layers, our mind clears the outer layers to make room for the new - and we have forgotten what we just learned.

Of course, this is not to say that you should jump up and down from your desk like a yo-yo. But a five minute break every half hour or so is a good idea.

4)    DON'T CRAM YOUR KNOWLEDGE INTO THE LAST FEW WEEKS.

Try to set up your routines as quickly as you can, leaving as much time as possible to digest the information (remember the onion.)

5)    THE NOTES YOU TAKE ARE CRUCIAL - IN TWO WAYS :
      a)    you can have too few, and

      b)    you can have too many.

A good way to decide what is too much and what is too little is to imagine yourself the night before the exam. You are trying, say, to remember the key parts of the reign of Richard III. You open your notes to find that you have only the word 'Hunchback' written down. Unless the question relates to Anatomy in the Reign of Richard III, you are in trouble.

At the other extreme, you can have 50 pages of notes discussing the merits and demerits of this remarkable man.  You may have written the world's best notes on Richard's introduction of the 'habeus corpus' - the right of a person to get out of gaol on bail.  Unfortunately, there is just NOT ENOUGH TIME TO READ THEM!!

So somewhere between these two, there lies the best way for YOU to make notes.  And it is not something that can be taught to you by someone else. *YOU WILL HAVE TO FIND OUT WHAT WORKS FOR YOU BY TRIAL AND ERROR.*  And that means that you will make many mistakes before you get it right.  And that means that you should start NOW.

6)    USE KEY-WORDS.

Thus when dealing with Richard III, you may use the words 'habeus corpus' and 'Princes in the Tower'.  If you have read your work well, using the techniques of concentration and so on, these two key words may be all you need to bring back all the rest of Richard's story (the habeus corpus is a major breakthrough in British legal history, a breakthrough in mercy as well as law; the Princes in the Tower refers to the common belief perpetuated by Shakespeare that Richard killed the two rightful child heirs to the throne. Together these two ideas seem to contradict each other.)

7)    HOW TO REMEMBER LISTS OF KEY-WORDS.

The problem boils down to this :  the key words of a particular topic will form a list - therefore how do you learn lists?

There are several ways :

a)    *YOU CAN FORM A RHYME CONTAINING THE INFORMATION.*  e.g. *In fourteen hundred and ninety two, Columbus sailed the ocean blue.*  It's not much but once heard, it will never be forgotten.

b)    *YOU CAN TAKE THE FIRST LETTERS OR SYLLABLES OR EACH WORD AND MAKE UP A NONSENSE WORD WITH THOSE LETTERS.*  e.g. SOHCAHTOA is a common one to remember the definitions of sine, cosine and tangent in trigonometry.

c)    *YOU CAN FORM A SENTENCE USING THE REQUIRED INFORMATION AS THE FIRST LETTER OF THE WORDS IN THE SENTENCE.*  e.g.  You may wish to learn the planets of the solar system in order :

Mercury, Venus, Earth, Mars, Jupiter, Saturn, Uranus, Neptune, Pluto.

A sentence to remember this could be :

*Men Very Easily Make Jugs Serve Useful Needs and Pleasures.*

d)    *PROFESSIONAL MEMORY EXPERTS,* the ones you sometimes see on television reciting lists of hundreds of names that they have only just seen, often use a rhyming device together with numbers.

i)    THUS FIRST THEY LEARN THE TABLE BELOW (ON THE LEFT).  Notice that each word rhymes with its corresponding number.  Hence it is very easy to remember.

| 1 | sun | *nutrition* |
|---|-----|-------------|
| 2 | shoe | *safety* |
| 3 | tree | *payment* |
| 4 | door | *education* |
| 5 | hive | *investigation* |
| 6 | sticks | *punishment* |
| 7 | heaven | *investment* |
| 8 | gate | *university* |
| 9 | wine | *parents* |
| 10 | hen | *mechanics* |

Now, imagine that we have to memorise the list on the right.

ii)    THE SECOND THING TO DO IS TO RELATE THE WORD "SUN" WITH THE WORD "NUTRITION".  To do this you must do two things :  use as much imagery as you can, and make sure YOU fit in the picture.

So you might think of a balanced diet to give you NUTRITION.  You know that fresh air and sunshine are necessary, so you imagine yourself lying under a hot sun soaking up the nutrition.  Feel the sun's rays on your back, feel how hot it is and so on and all the while remember that the sun is providing you with nutrition.  The more vivid you can make the picture, the easier it will be to remember that "nutrition" goes with "sun" and "sun" is the first on the list, because it rhymes with "1".

iii)  NEXT DO THE SAME THING WITH THE SECOND WORD ON EACH LIST - "shoe" and "safety".  And so on down the list.

iv)    WHEN YOU HAVE FINISHED THE LIST, check through to see that you can remember each item.  If you can't remember number 7 say, it means that you have not used your image making properly.  Go through number 7 again, reinforcing the image.

v)     THEN GO THROUGH THE LIST AGAIN AND AGAIN UNTIL YOU ARE SATISFIED THAT YOU KNOW EACH ONE.

Then give yourself a test :  write down the list forwards then backwards.  You will find that this is remarkably easy.  Ask someone to quiz you on the list in any order.  It will seem easier to do each time.

vi)    BUT DON"T BECOME COMPLACENT!!

The next day, try the same exercise.  It will be just as easy.

Wait a week, and go through the list again.  This time you will probably find that you will not be as fast.  You won't forget any words on the list, but it will take you a few times before you are as confident as you were a week ago.

Now is the time to reinforce the list.  Go through your images again, concentrating actively as you did the first time.  This will reinforce your list so that you could go for perhaps a week.  Revise it at the end of that week and it will be yours for perhaps 3 weeks.  Revise it again at the end of those 3 weeks and it will stay with you for a month.  By then, you will have probably finished the course.  If not, you know what to do.

IF YOU HAVE NOT YET TRIED THIS METHOD, YOU SHOULD DO SO
NOW - OTHERWISE IT IS HARD TO BELIEVE THE CLAIMS I WILL
MAKE ABOUT IT.

a)     Once you are convinced that this list-image method works, you will
no doubt have come up with some objections - like *"That's great for
one list, but what if I have more than one - like 50?"*

That's O.K. too.  Your memory is remarkable.  This same process can be
used again and again on different lists WITHOUT THE LISTS BECOMING
MIXED UP!!!

I once learned 50 lists of 10 words each to see if it could be done.
A friend chose the words at random from a dictionary.  In a single
night I learned the 50 lists and could recite the 500 items back in
any order!!  This is truly the best way of learning lists.

b)     Another objection is that lists may be quite common in subjects
like History (the causes of the First World War, etc.), but the
subjects that cause the most trouble - maths and science perhaps -
can't be 'listified'.  That's fair enough, and you may not be able to
condense some subjects into lists.  But it may be that you haven't
tried to make lists in maths because you didn't know how to remember
the lists.

Now that you do, you may try to make lists in all subjects :  for
instance, you may have trouble in remembering how to add fractions.
But you could certainly make a list of the steps needed and then
remember the list of steps.

c)     Or you may have to know 20 theorems for geometry.  Just make a
list.

d)     Or if you are doing higher maths, you will have to know algorithms
for almost everything.  (An algorithm is just a set of steps that you
remember in order to do a particular task - e.g. the long division and
long multiplication algorithm).  And every algorithm consists of a
number of steps in a given order.  The problem in higher mathematics
is that nearly everything is in algebra and hence is difficult to
associate with sun, shoe, etc.  But each algebraic step can be
DESCRIBED by an English word.

*For example, perhaps you have a test on solving equations.  Now the
hard part is that there seem to be so many types of equations.  But the
teacher always seems to remove any fractions first.  Then to expand any
brackets, then to collect like terms, then to get the unknowns to one
side and the numbers to the other, then to solve the equation.*

*Well then here's your list :*

> *fractions*
> *brackets*
> *collect*
> *one side*
> *solve*

And before you object that there are other types of equations that need
other techniques, don't forget that you could make lists for these too.

e)    THE POINT IS THAT VIRTUALLY ANY SUBJECT CAN BE LISTIFIED, AND ANY LIST CAN BE MEMORISED.

8)   TRY TO SEE WHAT THE ENTIRE CHAPTER IS ABOUT BEFORE YOU TRY TO LEARN IT.

Thus if you have to learn a chapter for a History test, and the chapter has a summary, then read the summary carefully BEFORE YOU READ THE CHAPTER.

Many courses - maths and science in particular - are designed so that you have to study for years before you can see the use of what you are studying.

*IF YOU CAN, YOU SHOULD ALWAYS TRY TO GET AN OVERVIEW OF WHAT YOU ARE GOING TO DO BEFORE YOU DO IT.*  You then know what to look for, and can start fitting the new knowledge into place as you are reading.  This leads on to the next section :

9)   ALWAYS STUDY WITH A PEN IN YOUR HAND.

As you read you should make a habit of marking important parts of your book. *YOU SHOULD JOT DOWN POINTS THAT YOU THINK IMPORTANT OR THAT YOU DON'T UNDERSTAND SO THAT WHEN YOU COME TO SUMMARISE, MOST OF YOUR WORK IS ALREADY DONE.*

In subjects where DIAGRAMS occur - as in geometry, chemistry, biology and geography for example - you should practise these regularly.  All it takes is a few minutes to see if you can reproduce a diagram, and the benefit is obvious.

*(Incidentally, if you wish to eat while studying, then eat something that will leave both hands free - I guess that leaves you with gum only - but the distraction of opening a packet of chips, say, is not worth it.  As well as distraction, you can't make notes at the same time.)*

10)  STATE KEY POINTS ALOUD.

Some of us have a memory that works best when we input information visually - i.e. by reading.  But some learn best by hearing information, as in a class lesson.  Sometimes, information that is both seen AND heard is retained better than if we just read it or just hear it.

*THUS, ONCE YOU HAVE A LIST OF KEY POINTS, READ IT ALOUD.*

11)  EXPECT YOUR LEARNING TO SPEED UP AND SLOW DOWN.

When just starting a new topic, we generally start learning very quickly. However, as we learn more, our rate of learning may slow down as we then have more things with which to compare and contrast the new work.

This of course can be very discouraging unless we are aware of what is happening.  It may be no more than we are tired.  But it is more likely to mean that our subconscious mind is consolidating our new knowledge, is filing it away where we can recall it easily and is making associations and comparisons with our old knowledge.

*A SHORT REST OR BRIEF EXERCISE FOLLOWED BY A RENEWED ATTACK ON THE WORK IS THE BEST REMEDY.  Whatever else, don't be discouraged and don't put it off. PERSISTENCE IS THE NAME OF THE GAME!!*

12)  REST OR SLEEP AFTER YOU HAVE STUDIED.

Many experiments confirm that the best results are obtained if you follow this pattern.  The mind seems to have an almost limitless ability to absorb knowledge, BUT AT ITS OWN RATE.  If you try to cram new knowledge in too quickly, the previous knowledge seems to be crowded out.  *A short break, even a five minute rest in your chair is time well spent.*

13)  YOU MUST REVISE.

As you saw in the list-image method, memory will always need reinforcing at regular intervals no matter how good your memory technique.  There is nothing you can substitute for revision.  It must be done.

There are two questions to be borne in mind about revision :

a)    WHEN to revise, and

b)    HOW to revise.

a)    The WHEN question depends on you.

You may have an ability to memorise a list of words and need NEVER revise them in order to recall them.  If you are such a person then skip to section 14.

If you are an ordinary mortal however, you will find that the list you memorised today will be able to be recalled in a week's time - but you will find it difficult to do so.  If, after a fortnight, you have not revised and reinforced a list, you will almost certainly forget at least part of it.  As I said before, people will vary in how long they can retain a list before they forget it.  But, as a guide :

If you learn it today and revise it tomorrow, you will remember it for a week.

If at the end of the week you revise it again, going over the images in the same way as when you first memorised it, you will remember it with ease for the next week.

Revise at the end of that week and it is your's for 3 more weeks.

Revise at the end of that period and it is your's for the next month.

If, during this time you have formed associations with the knowledge, if you have used the knowledge in homework and so on, then it will probably remain your's for life.

b)    The HOW question will obviously depend on what subject you are studying.

But one thing is certain :  you must have notes ready to study when the time comes.  *Your lists must have been prepared already.*  It is a waste of time for you to revise the entire textbook on the night before the exam.

During the course, you should be making notes, summarising, memorising and so on as part of your nightly work.  Your study time can then be spent on expanding the notes you have taken, on comparing and contrasting with other ideas you will have and so on.  This is particularly so in maths and science and will be treated in detail in that chapter.

14) DON'T FORGET TO TALK ABOUT YOUR WORK WITH FRIENDS.

    i)    As you talk about your work to someone who is also doing your course, several beneficial things must happen :  you must recall the work, you must analyse it, you must answer questions about your own ideas, you must defend your ideas against criticism and so on.

          As well, your friends will give you different viewpoints and ideas about the work, you will find out what they think is important, where they were able to find information, etc.

          This aspect of study is often overlooked, as it is so easy to waste time spent with friends.  But if you are on guard against this, time spent in this manner is valuable.  (More will be said on this topic in the section on the private student.)

    ii)   Remember too the idea of the DEVIL'S ADVOCATE (playing the devil's advocate means to adopt the opposite point of view to that which you usually hold).

          *So that if, for instance, you have learned that one underlying cause of the Second World War is the Treaty of Versailles, argue that the Treaty had nothing to do with the war.*

          In doing this you will find that your knowledge is being tested by yourself.  You will find that the reasons for your belief are either strengthened (if you find it difficult to argue against them) or that you are able to critically examine the "experts" (if you find that some of the arguments against the Treaty are sound).  Either way your knowledge will be expanded.

# CHAPTER SIX

## WHAT TO DO IN CLASS OR LECTURE

SUMMARY

1....PURPOSES OF GROUP LESSONS

2....FIND OUT THE TOPIC BEFORE THE LESSON

3....LISTEN ACTIVELY

4....DON'T ACCEPT EVERYTHING AS BEING CORRECT

5....KEY-NOTES ON KEY-POINTS

There are many things you can do while sitting in front of a teacher or lecturer.

Everyone at some time drowses!! And generally there is a good reason - not the fact that there is a lack of oxygen in the room; this is the reason that is usually trotted out at staff-meetings but it is seldom the real reason. What people are afraid of saying in public, is that the lesson was boring with no redeeming features at all. That is the real reason and it is dreaded by all teachers and lecturers!!

The class room lesson, where the teacher speaks for forty to sixty minutes, is a very inefficient method of either promoting thought or transmitting facts. *IT TAKES NO ACCOUNT OF THE DIFFERENCES BETWEEN STUDENTS AND SINCE THEY JUST SIT, IT PRODUCES PASSIVE LISTENING.*

So why have such lessons?

1)   PURPOSES OF GROUP LESSONS.

   a)   *THE LESSON MAY GIVE YOU AN IDEA OF WHAT THE WHOLE TOPIC IS ABOUT.* As you have seen, the first thing you should try to do is to get this overview, and if the lesson can give you this it is worth while.

   b)   Most courses end with an exam. Exams have a tendency to repeat questions year after year. *THIS SORT OF KNOWLEDGE, I.E. WHAT TOPICS OR QUESTIONS ARE IMPORTANT,* is not generally found in textbooks. *BUT IT IS OFTEN STRESSED IN CLASSROOMS.*

   c)   *YOU MAY BE GIVEN HINTS ABOUT THE BEST TEXTS TO READ OR WHERE TO FIND ADDITIONAL MATERIAL TO EXTEND OR ILLUMINATE A PART OF THE COURSE.*

   d)   *THE TEACHER/LECTURER MAY GIVE YOU CONNECTIONS BETWEEN SEEMINGLY UNRELATED IDEAS.*

   *So in an astronomy class you may learn that the North Star gradually moved into its present position roughly 500 years ago. If no more is said then you have been given an unrelated fact - unrelated to anything. But you may have a teacher who mentions that without a North Star you cannot navigate at sea and therefore you would expect great ocean going voyages of exploration to commence about the same time. Hence "In fourteen hundred and ninety two, Columbus, etc. etc." This connection then reinforces two topics and may explain even more.*

So what should you do to get more out of a lesson?

2) **FIND OUT WHAT TOPIC IS TO BE COVERED BEFOREHAND.**

*KNOWING THIS, TRY TO DO SOME READING OR THINKING ABOUT THE TOPIC BEFORE THE LESSON OR LECTURE.* You may not have to ask the teacher what is to be covered next - it may be as simple as looking at the next few pages of the text.

So if you see that the next topic to be covered is "irregular verbs", you can skim the text to get the gist of the writing and can then approach the lesson knowing roughly what the text states as being important. *YOU WILL FIND THAT YOUR UNDERSTANDING INCREASES IF THE TOPIC IS NOT ALTOGETHER STRANGE TO YOU.* (As the simplest of examples, you may have learned how the regular verbs go. You may understand perfectly. But you come to class the following day a few minutes late. You sit down and find that the class is still discussing verbs. You relax because you know that you know the rules for verbs.

Suddenly you realise that the rules today are NOT the rules from yesterday. Immediately your self-confidence is shaken and worse still your confidence in your ability to learn is gone. You may not find out that today's lesson is on irregular verbs - verbs that DON'T follow the normal rules - until it is too late. Coming early to class may have helped, but too often you will find that teachers don't stress that today's work is the exception to yesterday's. Such teachers seem to believe in all students' ability to mind-read.)

3) **LISTEN ACTIVELY.**

That is listen for key words, for breaks in the argument (the 'oh that reminds me ...' type), listen for 'therefore', 'hence', 'on the other hand' and so on. *TRY TO SEE WHAT THE TEACHER IS DRIVING AT, WHAT THE OVERALL ARGUMENT IS AND TRY TO CONCENTRATE ON THE MAIN THEME OF THE LESSON* rather than getting bogged down in details. Details can be filled in later.

4) **DON'T ACCEPT EVERYTHING YOU HEAR AS BEING 100% TRUE.**

   i) *CRITICISE THE ARGUMENT PRESENTED* - e.g. don't panic when the rules for verbs appear to be broken. Just make a note that there seems to be a contradiction from yesterday. If you can, ask about it then and there, but if you cannot, see the teacher as soon as possible after the class.

   ii) *TRY TO DISTINGUISH BETWEEN FACT AND OPINION* - if it is fact, then who says so? An unsupported fact is useless except as a debating topic.

5) **MAKE KEY-NOTES ON KEY-POINTS.**

Key points remind you of the arguments that you have heard. These can be filled out later for study purposes. *READ YOUR NOTES, THINK ABOUT THEM AND FILE THEM AS SOON AS POSSIBLE AFTER YOU GET HOME.*

Read your notes, think about them and file them as soon as possible after you get home. Make added notes to yourself on points that you don't understand or think of as vital. And remember that you will need these notes the night before the exam - *SO THEY MUST BE ABLE TO BE READ EASILY.*

# CHAPTER SEVEN

## HOW TO STUDY MATHS AND SCIENCE

SUMMARY

1....THE GOLDEN RULE - TREASURE YOUR MISTAKES

2....WHAT IS A MISTAKE

3....HOW TO LIST MISTAKES

4....WHAT TO DO WHEN YOU 'FAIL' AN EXAM

5....USE TEACHERS, FRIENDS, THE WORLD AS RESOURCE CENTRES

6....THE PERSONALISED SUMMARY - AND ITS UPDATES

7....WORDS AND PHRASES WORTH LISTENING FOR

8....ADDITIONAL LISTS AND QUESTIONS TO HELP

9....CONCLUSION AND COMMON MYTHS

This section is larger than the others.  This is not coincidence.  Nor is it that I think that maths and science are harder to study than other subjects.  The section is larger because of the terrible ideas that people have on how to study maths and science - from 'you can't study maths and science' to 'you've either got a mathematical brain or you haven't'.

Misconceptions in this area make the study of maths and science terribly difficult.  Here I have spelled out a step by step approach based on a single idea :

### WHAT TO DO WITH MISTAKES

Since you can argue that mistakes are at the basis of all subjects, what is said here can be used in the study of all subjects.

Thus this is a book within a book and you should read it whether you are doing maths or not.  There will be no heavy mathematical examples, only techniques of effective study that you can use in any subject.

1)    THE GOLDEN RULE - TREASURE YOUR MISTAKES.

Schools teach us many things.  One thing that ALL schools teach however, is that it is GOOD to get questions right and that it is BAD to get them wrong. This is taught to us right from Kindergarten, where we got a star on our books for GOOD work and nothing otherwise.

We can all remember the day the teacher smiled at us and said :  "Good work" or "That's right" just as we can remember the time the teacher frowned and said :  "That's bad" or "That's wrong".

The result of this is that we grow up being ASHAMED of our mistakes. When our tests are handed back in class, we turn them upside-down so that no-one can see how many mistakes we have made.

Some students will even tear their test paper up so that the evidence is destroyed!

So great is this feeling of shame that some students have committed suicide over a bad exam result.

What I wish you to consider here is this ;

A)    WE CAN ONLY LEARN FROM OUR MISTAKES.

B)    WE CAN ONLY IMPROVE BY STUDYING WHERE WE WENT WRONG.

C)    WE WILL LEARN VERY LITTLE FROM THE MISTAKES OF OTHERS.

D)    WE WILL LEARN VERY LITTLE IF WE ADOPT THE STUDY TECHNIQUES OF OTHERS - I.E. WE MUST DEVELOP OUR OWN.

E)    WE WILL LEARN NEXT TO NOTHING IF THE WORK DOES NOT SEEM TO APPLY TO US.

But of these statements, one stands out as being the *GOLDEN RULE OF STUDENTS* :

## WE ONLY LEARN FROM OUR MISTAKES

To make doubly sure let's change it to :

## TREASURE YOUR MISTAKES

The background to this is easy to see ....

How many times have you understood something and your friend didn't?  And the next day, your friend understood something which you could not?

Now if you both sat for a test the following day, it could happen that you both got the SAME MARK - but that you each make DIFFERENT MISTAKES!!

So if you tore your paper up in disgust or shame or anger, you would never find out *how to remedy your mistake*.  If on the other hand, your friend kept the exam paper, and found out how to fix the mistake that he or she made, then the next test - look out for your friend!!

Let's get back to our Golden Rule :

## TREASURE YOUR MISTAKES

Now it's all very well to say this, but how are you supposed to treasure them?

Do you ring up your friends and tell them?  If you do you won't have your friends long.

Do you tell your parents about them?  You can try but even the best of parents will stop you sooner or later.

How about tackling this problem from a different angle?

CONSIDER THIS QUESTION ....

What would you like to have in front of you on the night before the BIG EXAM?

After making the usual jokes (my teacher, my priest, etc.) most students think seriously about this question.

I have asked students the same question for years and it is surprising how many give the same answer!

You've probably guessed it - most students would like a list of their OWN past mistakes, with the corrections shown, of course.

*THE BENEFITS OF HAVING YOUR OWN PAST MISTAKES IN FRONT OF YOU ARE OBVIOUS :*

i)      *FIRSTLY,* you can see if the SAME mistake occurs consistently.

        *For instance, in a mathematics class, the current work in Cartesian geometry (using the X-Y axes), may require you to solve simple equations. This may be a weak point of yours and hence you make many mistakes. You may believe that you cannot 'do geometry' when in fact it is a part of algebra that is your problem. If you had written down the fact that you could not solve equations WHEN YOU WERE STUDYING EQUATIONS YOU WOULD NOW PERCEIVE THE OBVIOUS - LEARN EQUATIONS OR ELSE!!*

        Remember, if you did not make a note of the mistake, you may think that you could do neither algebra nor geometry!

ii)     *SECONDLY,* you can SEE THE MISTAKES THAT YOU HAVE MADE - not the mistakes that the author of the 'study guide' made when he/she was at school, NOR the mistakes that your teacher thinks you will make, NOR the mistakes that the person alongside you made NOR the mistakes that Einstein made - all of which are of little use to you, BUT the mistakes that YOU have made.

iii)    *THIRDLY,* you can SEE HOW TO FIX THE MISTAKES because, since you TREASURE YOUR MISTAKES, you would have listed the correct solutions with the mistakes.

2)  WHAT IS A MISTAKE?

It may seem a little late to ask this question but you'd be surprised at the different reactions that people have when they start to list their mistakes.

a)      Some list only the mistakes they made in tests.

b)      Some list the 'big' mistakes - i.e. mistakes that were 'important' in their eyes.

c)      Some list the mistakes that the teacher said were important - whether they made them or not.

d)      And some decide that one mistake was just 'careless' but that another mistake wasn't, and then list the non-careless mistakes.

i)      LET'S LOOK AT THE 'CARELESS' MISTAKES FIRST - since they are the most common of them all.

        Each of us at some stage will work through a problem, get all the working right, but in the last line may say 2 + 2 = 7. We get the paper back, see that our mistake was a 'careless' one and forget it, sure in the knowledge that we understood the problem and that we 'would never make that mistake again'.

And you won't!!

Next time you'll possibly say 2 + 2 = 9 or 21 or something else.  And each time you do you'll lose marks.  And each time you'll say it was a careless mistake and do nothing about it!!

From now on let us forget the whole concept of careless mistakes - THERE ARE ONLY MISTAKES - THAT'S ALL!!

So if you write 2 + 2 = 7, treat it just as seriously as any other mistake.

*Ask yourself, 'how did I make this mistake?'*

*Am I going too fast?*

*Should I check my work?*

*Is there a quick way to check my work?*

*Since I've made this mistake so many times, should I use a calculator, even for these 'easy' ones?*

*Did I become distracted during this question?*

*Was I worrying about the next question or running out of time to cause the mistake?*

*Is my writing clear, or did I read the second 2 as a 5?*

*Do I need glasses?*

There are many more reasons that you can ask, and until you do, until you take ALL mistakes seriously, you will not improve.

ii)    And while we are on the subject - *DON'T FOOL YOURSELF!!!*

Nothing is more irritating than someone who goes through life deceiving himself/herself.

We all do it at some stage, but the moral is 'To thine own self be true'.

And it is very easy to fool yourself in maths and science.  Many students get sold on the idea of TREASURING MISTAKES  but when they start to do exercises .... well, does this sound familiar?

You check the answers in the back of the book or wherever, and find that you got a problem wrong.  You change the answer to the right one, tick it, and go on with the next problem!!  You may even say 'Oh, I see' as if that will make any difference in a month's time when you sit for an exam on the topic.

If you have never done this then keep up the good work.  If you have, then now is the time to stop.

iii)  Whatever you do, don't kid yourself!!

IF YOU DON'T FIX YOUR MISTAKES AS SOON AS POSSIBLE, YOU'LL MAKE THEM
AGAIN AND AGAIN.

So what is a mistake?

ANYTHING.  ANYTHING YOU GET WRONG!!!!

4)    HOW TO LIST MISTAKES

There is no one way of listing your OWN mistakes.  First I will list a few
successful methods I have seen.  You may choose one of these, but you will
quickly adapt it to suit yourself - remember, you are doing this FOR YOURSELF
- it is YOU who will need them the night before the big exam, it is YOU who
will be using the list to find out and remedy your weaknesses, so of course
you should tailor it to your own needs.

METHOD 1)    *Imagine you are doing a course in algebra.  As you go through the
course you come across different topics - algebraic expressions,
algebraic fractions, removal of brackets, solving equations, and
so on.  Some students rule columns with headings for each part of
the course, and when a mistake is made, enter the mistake in the
appropriate column.*

This has the benefit of having all your mistakes in front of you for the
particular course.

The problem is to fit all the mistakes on the paper, and to have room for the
corrections as well.  Also, many of the mistakes you make won't be algebraic
mistakes - they'll be arithmetic ones like 2A + 2A = 7A.  So in your list of
mistakes you must provide columns for arithmetic mistakes.

A variation of this technique uses the columns but lists only the page number
and question number that you got wrong.  This overcomes the space problem,
but makes it harder to find the mistake.  Remember, the night before the BIG
exam you won't have time to go backwards and forwards from book to book.

METHOD 2)    *I first saw this approach used by a student who loved writing
notes to himself.  His method evolved into a diary approach ...*

*'Dear Diary, Today I was an IDIOT.  I made the same mistake in
adding fractions that I made yesterday...'*

*He would then go on to describe the mistake, how it fitted in with
other similar mistakes and so on.*

*As well as listing mistakes, he would write encouragement notices
to himself.  'At last I can solve equations, etc.'*

The benefits of this scheme are that it is totally personal - as are your
mistakes and progress.  The drawback is that firstly it takes time to write
your diary, and time may be short.  Secondly, this student had no way of
seeing whether his mistakes were forming a pattern - which Method 1 gives you.

METHOD 3)    *Some students mark their mistakes in their textbooks, and later
copy them into a special book.*

But whatever you do, one thing comes out of this section :

*YOU NEED A LIST OF YOUR OWN PAST MISTAKES - AND YOU NEED THEM IN CATEGORIES - I.E. SO THAT YOU CAN SEE WHERE YOUR MISTAKES REALLY LIE.*

If you faithfully follow only this first directive, TREASURE YOUR MISTAKES, you will find that you are taking an active interest in your work rather than just sitting back and waiting for that wonderful day when you wake up and can get 100% in a maths or science test.    You will find two examples of listing your mistakes in the Glossary.

4)     WHAT TO DO WHEN YOU 'FAIL' AN EXAM

Unless you are a gifted student, sooner or later you will fail a test.  With your new attitude of TREASURING YOUR MISTAKES, you should react in much the same way as if you passed - i.e. you should list your mistakes, knowing that you won't learn unless you fix them.

Think of a student (you, maybe) working through a particular topic.  The one thing the student NEVER knows, is NEVER sure about, is 'WHAT IS IMPORTANT?' Is it any wonder that people fail tests?  You may have studied the wrong part of the topic, as well as not understanding other parts.  Bear this in mind when you get a low mark -

i)     *THE TEST HAS JUST SHOWN YOU WHAT IS, AND WHAT IS NOT IMPORTANT.*

ii)    *THE TEST HAS JUST GIVEN YOU WORKED EXAMPLES OF ALL THOSE QUESTIONS YOU CAN'T DO.*

iii)   *THE TEST HAS JUST DIRECTED YOUR ATTENTION TO YOUR OWN AREAS OF WEAKNESS.*

iv)    *THE TEST HAS JUST SHOWN YOU WHERE YOUR UNDERSTANDING IS LACKING.*

- all of these are the BEST study guides you could ask for!!

What you do with them is now up to you.  You can be like the students mentioned above, tear up the test in shame, or as I would like you to do :

*LIST AND CATEGORISE YOUR MISTAKES!!*

5)     USE TEACHERS, FRIENDS, THE WORLD AS RESOURCE CENTRES

Having listed your mistakes, however, what do you then do?

Well, you've obviously got to find out how to fix them.  But how?

If you think that your teacher is going to fix them all for you - think again.

*LET'S GET A FEW FACTS ON TEACHERS AND TEACHING STRAIGHT FIRST :*

i)     MOST TEACHERS ARE KEEN THAT YOU DEVELOP YOUR SKILLS IN THEIR SUBJECT. I have never met a teacher who deliberately set out to confuse students. But, in the average class, there may be about 30 students.  The class may last for, say 45 minutes.  That gives, say, 15 minutes for the teacher to explain the subject matter on the board, leaving 1 minute for each student to be helped individually!!  Now in your minute, what can the teacher do to help you?

In this one minute, can the teacher perceive that your trouble is not with the work that you are doing now?  That your trouble really lies in not being able to add fractions, say, which you did 2 years ago?

The chances are slim.

ii)    REMEMBER TOO, THAT WHILE TEACHERS MAY BE ABLE TO SEE YOU AT LUNCHBREAK, that you will have to join the queue with other students seeking help.  Also the teacher may be busy with staff meetings, with supervision rosters and so on.

iii)   TO OVERCOME THIS, YOUR FIRST JOB IS TO EXPLAIN TO YOUR TEACHER WHAT YOUR STUDY METHOD IS!!  In this way the teacher will understand why, for instance, you are asking a question about adding fractions (year 5 work) in a year 9 algebra class.

If your study method has been explained, the teacher will also take a greater interest in guiding you through your troubles.  You'll find that your time in class will be better spent knowing that you can help the teacher help you, just by showing him or her where you need help.  Very quickly you'll gain that sense of purpose that comes in knowing that you are in control of your own learning.  Try it!!

iv)    HOWEVER, IT WILL CERTAINLY HAPPEN AT SOME TIME, THAT THE TEACHER JUST DOESN'T HAVE TIME TO GET AROUND TO YOU.  At 1 minute per student, what would you expect?  The average student (you - before you read this), will leave the question until the next lesson.  And of course, the next lesson is devoted to the next part of the course which you have trouble understanding because you didn't get to ask your question the day before.  And so it goes.  Very shortly, you can't understand the entire topic.  Even listing your mistakes is hard since you won't know where to put them.  What to do??

v)     OBVIOUSLY, YOU MUST FIX MISTAKES AS SOON AS THEY HAPPEN.  Leaving them for the next class is not good enough.  But if you can't ask the teacher then who?

My suggestion to you is very simple :

*Ask the person alongside you.*

*Ask the class 'brain'.*

*Ask your parents that night.*

*Ask another teacher at lunch-break.*

*Ask ANYONE!!*

I'm sorry if you expected some magic wand to be waved.  But this is the best advice in the world :

KNOWLEDGE IS WHERE YOU FIND IT !

Teachers aren't the only ones who have it - no matter what we tell you.  You may have a text-book - try reading it.  It may explain everything.  Try your local library after school.  Almost certainly there will be someone there who can help you.  And last, don't forget that YOU can probably figure it out YOURSELF - given the time.  But don't, DON'T put it off!!

So the next directive is :

*USE YOUR TEACHER, YOUR FRIENDS, YOUR WORLD AS RESOURCE CENTRES.*

**6)    THE PERSONALISED SUMMARY - AND ITS UPDATES.**

i)    Let's return for a moment to the night before the BIG EXAM.  As before let's ask the question *'WHAT WOULD YOU LIKE TO HAVE WITH YOU?'*

The list of past mistakes we have spoken of.  But there are other things as well.

Surely you would need a summary of the course!!  Like the one you would buy as a study guide in any bookshop and which I would advise against!!

Yes, you would need a summary of the course - but there the similarity ends.

ii)   Imagine that the course was on elementary geometry - and that one thing that you had to know was the formula for the area of a rectangle $A = L \times B$.

Now it would be best to keep the formulae in a special book.  And it would be best to give a worked example to illustrate how the formula works.

*QUESTION : Where to get the worked example?*

*ANSWER :    You know the answer - from your list of past mistakes!*

You can imagine setting it out :

At the top of the page you'd have the formula.

Next, you'd have a (correct) worked example, taken from your list of corrected mistakes.

And finally, you could have the same example but this time showing the mistake that you made when you did it in the test.  You may have got it wrong several times - if so include them.  You may have been told a useful trick to help in doing this type of problem - if so write it down.  In fact, you can keep ALL handy hints under the one heading. You can write notes to yourself using the Dear Diary approach.

*WHEN YOU HAVE FINISHED, YOU WILL HAVE YOUR OWN PERSONALISED STUDY GUIDE* that will explain your own problems with this formula $A = L \times B$, that will show the correct procedure for explaining it to YOU, and which will be totally devoted to your own development.  In fact, if you have done your summary well, your friends will gain very little from reading it - since it is *BASED ON YOUR MISTAKES AND YOUR LEARNING EXPERIENCES.*

iii)  Now, you will start with the heading $A = L \times B$, but you will probably make your first mistake at a later time.  Your next mistake using this formula may be a year later.  Or you may only ever make one mistake using it, or you may make many.

Therefore, if you are going to record your mistakes you will need an expandible folder into which you can add extra leaves as you need them. The moral is : there is always one more mistake that you will make - leave space for it!!

The next directive is therefore :

*MAKE YOUR OWN PERSONALISED SUMMARY AS YOU MEET NEW TOPICS, AND KEEP IT UP TO DATE.*

7)    WORDS AND PHRASES WORTH LISTENING FOR.

During your school career, you will spend a lot of time in class.  Most of this time you will spend 'learning and doing' mathematics or science - or whatever.

Your teacher will say things, do things and so on.  You will probably be asked to sit and watch, answer questions or do exercises.  This much you know.

i)    *BUT YOU CAN HELP YOURSELF IMMENSELY, BY LEARNING TO LISTEN FOR A FEW KEY WORDS.*

These are words that ALL teachers use to signal to you that what they are about to say is important.  What!!  Did you think that everything the teacher said was important!? Not so!   Teachers like to think it is, but I'm afraid not.

ii)    *TAKE AN EXAMPLE :*

*STUDENT A wishes only to be able to pass the BIG EXAM so that he can drop mathematics altogether.*

*STUDENT B wishes to be an engineer and to teach engineering at tertiary level.*

*STUDENT C wishes to be an historian.*

These three students are all in the same algebra class.

The subject is quadratic equations (some of you will have met this subject, some won't - don't worry either way.)  The teacher, say, starts the topic with the development of equations, then the need for quadratic equations in the 11th Century that led to their invention, then to the problems that were faced because of the fact that algebra had hardly been invented, then to the original methods used to solve them, then to the need for quick solutions to them in today's world, then to the relation of them to physics and projectiles, then to their solution by formula, then to how to derive the formula, then to examples in which the formula is needed, then to exercises for you to do, then to writing computer programs to solve them.

*Now tell me :  do you think that what is important for Student A will be the same for B or C and vice versa?*

Obviously not!!  So what to do?

Well, the three different students will make different notes.  That's O.K.  But no matter what your interests, there are still things that each student MUST take down.  That's where the KEY WORDS come in.

What are they?

iii)  Sooner or later your teacher will use such words as :

   a)    STANDARD QUESTION

   b)    TYPICAL EXAM QUESTION

   c)    SPECIAL USE OF THIS PROBLEM

   d)    WORKED EXAMPLE

There will be variations on these, but start listening for them now.
Always take a note of them.  Always understand them.  Let's take an
example of each :

   a)    A STANDARD QUESTION is a question that often appears in exam
         papers in disguise or as part of another harder question.

         For instance :  *"Prove that the product of two consecutive (one
         after the other) numbers is always even."*  This is what I would
         call a standard question.  It is not a question that is
         necessarily asked regularly in exams, but you need to be able to
         understand how to do it so that you can do questions that do
         appear in exams.

   b)    A TYPICAL EXAM QUESTION is self explanatory.  As soon as your
         teacher tells you that a particular question is typical, he or
         she is simply drawing  on the experience  of previous exams.
         It would be foolish to ignore such advice.

         A typical exam question which uses our standard question, may
         be :  *"Prove that the product of three consecutive numbers is
         divisible by 6."*

   c)    A SPECIAL USE OF THIS QUESTION will generally surprise you.  It
         is a use that you wouldn't have expected.

         For instance, writing a computer program to find prime numbers is
         not too hard.  The problem is that such programs are generally
         very slow.  One of the first ways used to speed up such programs
         is to use the standard question above.  (Since prime numbers can
         never be even - except 2 - we need only test every second number
         to see if it's prime.  And if you don't think that's important,
         the security of the U.S. defence system is controlled by
         computers, and their security codes are based on prime numbers.
         Find the prime numbers that are used and you can destroy the
         system - or the world.)

   d)    A WORKED EXAMPLE is always worth the trouble of noting.  It will
         NEVER replace your own, but at this stage in the lesson you won't
         have made any mistakes to use.

THEREFORE :

*LISTEN FOR KEY WORDS THAT WILL PREFACE AN EXAMPLE OR PIECE OF ADVICE THAT -
IN THE TEACHER'S OPINION - MAY HELP YOU.*

8)    ADDITIONAL LISTS AND QUESTIONS TO HELP.

     i)     There is another device you may use to help you revise.  'Revision' is a dirty word among most students.  It means that tests are approaching, and, as we have seen, most students hate tests because they fear mistakes.

            However, there is another reason that 'revision' is not the most-loved word :  to most students, revising means that they must START summarising!!  And most students simply do not know how to go about it.  *I once had a student who completed his summary for the BIG EXAM on the night before the exam.  It wasn't that he started late, it was just that he literally copied out EVERY PAGE of theory and EVERY worked example from the text-books.  Wait for it - there were 664 pages in the text-books!!  (I counted them.)*

            You, on the other hand, should have kept your summary up to date since day 1.  You will have your past mistakes illustrating each formula, worked examples, special questions, typical exam questions  and the like, to further illustrate each formula - what else can there be to do but learn them?  And since you have been keeping this up to date daily, you will find that you will know most of your work anyway.

            So what else can there be?

     ii)    If you have seen the following device at work you will know how powerful it can be.  It is simply this :

            Each time you learn a new piece of work, write it on a (large) piece of paper headed DO YOU KNOW ....

            The list that follows will include every type of question that you could be asked, and every piece of information that you need to know.  For an elementary algebra/geometry class the list may look like :

            *DO YOU KNOW ....*

            *1)     how to complete the square*

            *2)     how to add any types of algebraic fraction*

            *3)     given two sides of a triangle how to find the third*

            *4)     the condition that a line should be a tangent to a circle*

            and so on.

            Ideally the list will be LONG as you continue to find new ways of asking an old question.  (If you have done Pythagoras' theorem, you should have noticed that there are literally dozens of questions that are based on it.  You will find that the dozens become hundreds very quickly.)

            The idea of such a list is simple :  it is to try to overcome that terrible feeling when we know our work, feel confident about a test, but flunk it because we forgot that such-and-such a theorem could be used in a particular way.  Notice I say 'forgot' - there will always be the case that you haven't seen before and you should expect that to happen.  In that case you need all your problem solving skills - here we are only dealing with how to study and organise what you HAVE seen.

iii) Those of you with computers may wish to put such a list on your
machine so that each time you run the program, the list is given to
you in a different order.

Hence, you should :

*LIST YOUR TOPICS AND FORMULAE IN SHORT FORM - RUN THROUGH IT
REGULARLY AS A QUICK REVISION.*

9)  CONCLUSION AND COMMON MYTHS.

Now you have seen a comprehensive way of studying maths and science, it is a
good time to return to the methods of study that most people use ....

*THESE ARE THE METHODS YOU SHOULD NOT USE :*

a)  *You can't really study maths (this is the most popular).*

b)  *All you can do is go over what you've done in class (most common in
science).*

c)  *What you do is copy out all the theory and learn that.*

d)  *You just do examples.*

e)  *Write down the theory and a worked example for each topic (I took this
from a popular study guide!!)*

You may have come across others.

*I REPEAT, ALL THE ABOVE ARE TO BE AVOIDED LIKE THE PLAGUE!!*

Having completed our TREASURE YOUR MISTAKES approach, you must notice
that all these so-called ways of study have two things in common :

1)  They take no account of YOU THE STUDENT - they seem to imply that all
students have the same problems.

2)  They offer no advice to aid YOU through the course.  Nowhere does it
say that you must constantly update your work/mistakes.  You could be
forgiven for thinking that 'study' is something you do the night
before the exam.

3)  And, I suppose, the worst thing they do is to get you to believe that
studying is easy!!  IT ISN'T.  Studying is very hard.  You must be
dedicated and want to do better - otherwise you'll let your studying
(listing mistakes, etc.) lapse and return to the bewildered state that
most students are normally in.

This is not to say that it doesn't get easier.  You will find that
updating and revising your work will become second nature to you -
but START IT NOW.  It will pay dividends in attitude and results.

## SUMMARY

Golden Rule :  TREASURE YOUR MISTAKES

1)  LIST YOUR MISTAKES IN CATEGORIES.

2)  USE YOUR TEACHER, YOUR FRIENDS, YOUR WORLD AS A RESOURCE CENTRE.

3)  MAKE YOUR OWN PERSONALISED SUMMARY AS YOU MEET NEW TOPICS, AND KEEP IT UP TO DATE.

4)  LISTEN FOR KEY-WORDS THAT WILL PREFACE AN EXAMPLE OR PIECE OF ADVICE THAT - IN THE TEACHER'S OPINION - MAY HELP YOU.

5)  LIST YOUR TOPICS AND FORMULAE IN SHORT FORM - RUN THROUGH IT REGULARLY AS A QUICK REVISION.


*YOU SHOULD COPY THE FOLLOWING FLOW CHART AND PIN IT ABOVE YOUR DESK.*

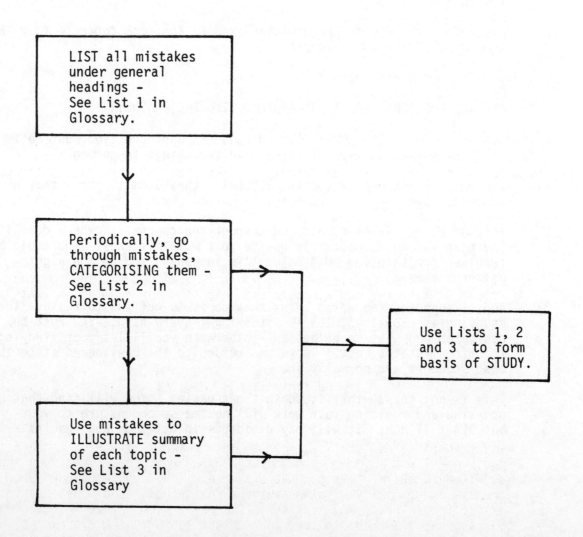

# CHAPTER EIGHT

# HOW TO WRITE ESSAYS

## SUMMARY

1....CHOOSE AND ORGANISE YOUR MATERIAL - MAIN THEME - PLANNING - SETTING OUT

2....ANALYSING AND DEVELOPING THE MAIN THEME

3....USING DETAILS TO SUPPORT THE MAIN THEME

4....USING EXAMPLES

5....USING COMPARISON AND CONTRAST

6....USING CAUSE AND EFFECT

7....GETTING THE DEFINITION CORRECT

8....ORGANISING THE ARGUMENT

9....SOME TECHNIQUES FOR COHERENCE

10...WHAT IS STYLE?

1)   CHOOSING AND ORGANISING MATERIAL

*A GOOD ESSAY MUST HAVE A PURPOSE.*  That is it must have an aim or be intended to do some particular thing - to make you laugh or cry, to inform you or to evoke some feeling within you.

a)   Your first task therefore is to decide precisely what it is you wish to say.  In other words, you must *DECIDE ON YOUR MAIN THEME.*

Imagine that you are to write an essay on trees.  Should you decide to write on their uses in building, their aesthetic value, how they grow, how many there are, their effect on the environment, or what? Your choice is imperative.  For once you have decided what your purpose is in writing the essay, you can then decide where to find material on that topic and so on.

b)   *YOUR NEXT STEP IS TO PLAN YOUR ESSAY.*  You have decided to write on the value of trees to the environment.  How then do you find your MATERIAL?  (Material is anything the writer uses to support his or her main theme.)

Thus, in this case you will need to know in what way trees enhance the environment and in what ways they are a menace.  Your first stop should be with yourself - have you had experiences that would support your theme, can you think of other persons that have shared your experiences or feelings?  Then you may like to seek help from a library.  Since your purpose is known to you, you can ask the librarian for specific help in finding reference material (nothing is more infuriating to librarians than to be asked "Do you have any books on trees?")

Once you have information, you can be more specific in developing your main theme :  you may come across the fact that trees act as air conditioners and air purifiers.  This may strike you as remarkable. Can you use this to state your main theme more specifically ....?

MAIN THEME :  *how to save on energy bills - and breathe clean air - by planting more trees.*

As you read or think about this theme you will find that you can start noting points that will support your theme with much greater ease than if you have no theme.

c)    IN THE FINAL ESSAY, YOUR FIRST SENTENCE WILL BE THE STATEMENT OF YOUR THEME.

In fact, the first paragraph may simply expand on the theme and its importance, your second paragraph would begin with your principal reason for supporting the theme, the third paragraph with your next reason, and so on.

2)    ANALYSING AND DEVELOPING THE MAIN THEME.

a)    'ANALYSIS' IS THE ART OF BREAKING DOWN A SUBJECT INTO ITS COMPONENT PARTS.

Development or examination of the component parts then allows the writer to argue for the main theme.

Thus while you feel strongly about trees and even that trees are good air conditioners, you should go further.  Why is having cool air desirable?  What about winter?  Will the presence of trees increase the moth and insect population?  Is it a bad thing if it does?  Will the roots of trees cause problems with plumbing?  If so, is it better to have the trees and an occasional bill for plumbing?  What does 'better' mean in this context?  Does it mean that money is the criterion?  If so, is money the only criterion?  And so on.

As you answer these points in your mind, always refer back to the main theme - is your answer relevant to the theme.

b)    ALWAYS RESIST THE TEMPTATION TO INCLUDE IRRELEVANT INFORMATION - NO MATTER HOW INTERESTING YOU FIND IT.

Such information will simply detract the reader's attention from your main theme.

3)    USING DETAILS TO DEVELOP A THEME.

WRITERS OFTEN USE SPECIFIC DETAILS TO SUPPORT THEIR THEME.

Thus you may support your air conditioner/tree argument by supplying the actual cost of running an average air conditioner for five years.  You should support these figures by supplying footnotes stating where and when you obtained the figures.

Having supplied the details you would then include a sentence or two showing how these figures relate to the main theme - "the figures show the high cost of air conditioning to the average householder ... "

4)    USING EXAMPLES.

*TO HIGHLIGHT A PARTICULAR IDEA, WRITERS OFTEN USE EXAMPLES.*

Once you have seen how an example can make an extremely difficult concept
clear, you will wonder why so many authors, particularly scientific authors,
don't use them.   Consider these two statements :

STATEMENT 1 :        *The erosion of the value of money over time causes great*
                     *hardship to persons on fixed incomes.*

STATEMENT 2 :        *My parents are retired and live on the pension.  Their*
                     *trouble is that prices keep on going up but their pension*
                     *doesn't.*

Either statement can mean the same, but how much easier is it to understand
the second than the first?   Because it includes an example.

5)    USING COMPARISON AND CONTRAST.

      a)    *WRITERS USE COMPARISON TO SHOW HOW TWO THINGS ARE SIMILAR - ESPECIALLY*
            *WHEN IT IS NOT OBVIOUS THAT THERE IS ANY SIMILARITY.*

            For instance, in the essay on trees, you would show the similarity
            between trees and air conditioners!

      b)    *ON THE OTHER HAND, CONTRAST IS USED TO SHOW HOW TWO SEEMINGLY SIMILAR*
            *THINGS ARE, IN FACT, DIFFERENT.*

            So that, having just shown that trees and air-conditioners are similar
            in the sense that they cool and purify the air, you could then show
            that they were totally UNLIKE each other as regards cost!!

These are two very powerful techniques that are easy to use.   You should look
for them in this or any other book and see how they bring a point home with
a minimum of fuss.

6)    USING CAUSE AND EFFECT.

      a)    *ANOTHER EASY TO USE BUT VERY POWERFUL WAY OF DEVELOPING YOUR THEME, IS*
            *TO SHOW HOW ONE EVENT CAUSES ANOTHER.*

            (The first event is called the 'cause' and the second event is called
            the 'effect' of the first event.)

            Thus, you may be able to show that why the Smith's always feel them-
            selves outdone by the Jones' is that the Jones' have more money to buy
            things because their energy fill is lower than the Smith's.  Any why?..
            because they don't have an expensive air conditioner, they have trees!

      b)    But you should be aware of two different types of causes : the
            NECESSARY and the SUFFICIENT ....

            *For example, clouds in the sky are necessary (i.e. needed or required)*
            *for rain, but having clouds in the sky doesn't mean that it is raining.*

            *On the other hand, if it is raining, then you are sure that there must*
            *be clouds in the sky - i.e. rain is sufficient to show that there are*
            *clouds in the sky (i.e. it's enough to know that it is raining to show*
            *that there must be clouds in the sky.)*

*Thus, in the example used, claiming a connection between Columbus and the North Star, the existence of the North Star is NECESSARY for Columbus' voyage but it was certainly NOT sufficient. He also needed money, crew, ability to lead, bravery, and so on.*

In using cause and effect, you will find many other pitfalls, but persevere in their use.

7)   GETTING THE DEFINITION CORRECT.

While you may be certain in your own mind of the meaning of the key word in your main theme, *YOU SHOULD ALWAYS CHECK TO SEE THAT THERE IS NO POSSIBLE AMBIGUITY.*

You should think also of who is going to read your essay : some persons may think that a tree is a large shrub perhaps; or that a tree is nothing smaller than a Canadian Redwood. Unlikely perhaps, but you can certainly think of cases where you thought one thing and someone else thought another. Much time and effort is saved by having an unambiguous meaning spelled out in the first paragraph.

If you make a habit of checking for meaning, you will often find that you are not sure in your own mind of the meaning of the simplest of words. If you are not, then how can you expect your readers to be?

8)   ORGANISING THE ARGUMENT.

a)   In mathematics you can have an algebraic argument that goes :

Line 1 implies
Line 2 which implies
Line 3 which implies
....
Line 9 which implies
Line 10 which is the conclusion.

Essay writing is definitely NOT like this. If you think you have an ironclad argument, rest assured that 'someone will shoot it down in flames.'

So with your tree argument, the best you can do is to present several points of view that relate to each other and support your main theme. Within each point you may be able to give some rigid logical connections but while there will be some connection between points it will never stand the test of the strict logician.

b)   This is not to say that you should not try to organise your arguments. On the contrary, that is a crucial part of your task. But if you try for strict logic you will only succeed if you narrow your main theme down to a trivial level.

The logic you should strive for would certainly contain the pros and cons for each argument. In this way you achieve a balance and also - to some extent - anticipate your critics.

c)   But the overriding consideration is this ; *YOUR ARGUMENT MUST BE CLEAR AND CONCISE TO THE READER* so that even if he or she disagrees with you, then the disagreement must be over facts rather than the argument.

Before leaving this section on organising the argument, you must have a rough idea of how to set out your essay.

*As stated in section 1c, your first paragraph - your introduction - will consist of your main theme and a statement of how you intend to argue.*

*Next, you would have the 'body' of the essay, consisting of your arguments, examples and so on.*

*Last you would have a conclusion, where you should restate your theme in the light of the arguments that you have presented.*

9)      SOME TECHNIQUES OF COHERENCE.

Even assuming that you are able to have a clear purpose and a good plan, there are techniques used by good writers to get everything to "hang together".  You will find that no matter which sentence you select, it will be related to the one before and the one after.  THIS IS COHERENCE, and is what all the preceding sections lead up to.  There are several techniques that you can use to help in achieving it.

a)      *TRY TO USE WORDS THAT SIGNAL TO THE READER THE CONNECTION BETWEEN IDEAS.*

Words like :

*therefore .... thus .... hence .... on the other hand*
*conversely .... secondly .... for example .... similarly*

These words and phrases tie ideas together or to the main theme of your essay.  They direct the reader's attention to the relationships that you are proposing.

b)      *BY REPEATING KEY-WORDS AGAIN AND AGAIN, THE READER'S ATTENTION IS DRAWN BACK TO THE MAIN THEME AND THE RELATIONSHIP OF THIS PARTICULAR SENTENCE TO IT.*

Key words and key ideas are used too seldom in many essays and while their absence can affect the reader, (by making the essay hard to follow), their absence can also affect the writer - YOU!

Thus, you may find that because you did not use a key word, that your own attention has wandered off the main theme and that you are including irrelevant material.  Thus the repetition of key words is valuable on at least two counts.

Of course the repetition of the same word again and again may irritate the reader.  An alternate method is to use another word or phrase with the same meaning.  For instance, instead of using the phrase 'key words' in the above paragraph, I could have used such phrases as :

*important words .... central ideas .... key notions*

You may use a thesaurus to help you find words that may be substituted for others.  Your librarian will show you how to use one.  (A word of warning however - it is unwise to change a simple word for a complex one.  Read the section on STYLE.)

But by whatever method, it should be tried.

c)    *CONSIDER THESE TWO SENTENCES :*

*"Trees cool the air.  They also provide oxygen at a very reasonable cost."*

We can connect these two sentences - i.e. provide coherence - by making a slight change ;

*"While cooling the air, trees provide oxygen at a very reasonable cost."*

Thus, the connection has been made by using the idea of time.  Both happen simultaneously.  You will come across many instances of this joining of sentences and many more where it may have been used to advantage.

d)    *IF YOU PRACTISE TRYING TO GET COHERENCE IN YOUR ESSAYS, YOU WILL CERTAINLY SUCCEED.*  Your writing may win no prizes for literature, but then no-one has won a prize for literature whose writing did not cohere.

## 10)  STYLE.

When two sentences have the same or similar meanings, but the type of English used in them is very different, we say that the sentences differ in 'STYLE'.

a)    So, if James Cagney, who immortalised himself on the screen playing gangster roles, had been born an Englishman 100 years earlier, we may have found him saying :

*"Sir, your features compel me to believe that you are related to an unhygenic rodent!!"*

How much more effective is Cagney's famous line :

*"YA DIRTY RAT !!!"*

b)    But go back and read the sentence above which starts 'So if James Cagney ...'

Notice that it is very long.

And notice that, while it is grammatically correct, it is hard to read.

c)    Here is another way of saying the same thing :

James Cagney is a movie star.
He immortalised himself on the screen by playing gangster roles.
However, if he had been born an Englishman 100 years earlier, his screen style would have been very different.
We would find him saying :
*"Sir, your features .... "*  and so on.

Notice that each new idea is given a sentence to itself. Notice that by doing so, the passage is easier to read - even though it contains the same ideas as the original.

d) Thus, the style you adopt in your essays, can affect the reader's comprehension.

    i) *IN GENERAL, YOU SHOULD TRY TO KEEP SENTENCES SHORT.*

    ii) *YOU SHOULD KEEP YOUR SENTENCES - AND WORDS - SIMPLE.*

    iii) *YOU SHOULD KEEP YOUR SENTENCES UNAMBIGUOUS - I.E. THEY SHOULD NEVER HAVE TWO MEANINGS.*

    iv) *YOU SHOULD GIVE EXAMPLES WHICH HIGHLIGHT THE POINT YOU WISH TO MAKE.*

    v) *YOU SHOULD AVOID SLANG - UNLESS YOU USE IT FOR EFFECT.*

    vi) *YOU SHOULD AVOID JARGON OR TECHNICAL TERMS - IF YOU NEED TO USE THEM, THEN DEFINE THEM FIRST.*

e) *FOLLOWING THE ABOVE GUIDELINES SHOULD HELP YOU ADOPT A LUCID STYLE.* Of course, great writers impose their own personality on their work, often breaking the rules that we lesser writers set up. By all means you should experiment with your writing. If we all adopted the same style, life would be dull indeed!

# CHAPTER NINE

## HOW TO STUDY LANGUAGES

SUMMARY

1....HOW TO DIVIDE A LANGUAGE

2....HOW TO READ A LANGUAGE

3....HOW TO WRITE A LANGUAGE

4....HOW TO LISTEN TO A LANGUAGE

5....HOW TO SPEAK A LANGUAGE

6....AS WELL AS ...

1)    HOW TO DIVIDE A LANGUAGE

*In studying any subject, you should always try to see if you can divide the subject into broad categories.*

Thus, it is customary to divide English up into Poetry, Drama, Literature and so on.  Dividing a subject up in this manner, allows you to develop the skills necessary for that part of the subject.  It's the same in playing tennis :  the skills you need in serving are not the same as the skills you need in receiving.

In the study of a foreign language, the rules are similar.  In general, there are four broad categories that must be mastered.  They are :

*READING .... WRITING .... LISTENING .... SPEAKING*

Now, depending on what course you are doing, you will find that the emphasis on each part changes.

i)    Thus, your first job is to find out what type of course you are doing! Sorry to bring up such an obvious point, but the subject FRENCH can mean many different things.  It's better to find out first.

ii)   If the emphasis is to be on writing the language, for instance, the GRAMMAR of the language will be far more important than if the emphasis is to be on SPEAKING the language.

      However, if you are studying LATIN, there is probably going to be little difference, since no-one speaks Classical Latin nowadays.

Let us examine the categories in turn.

2)   HOW TO READ A LANGUAGE

To develop skills in reading a foreign language, you must do exactly that :
READ IT!!

The problem that confronts most students is finding material to read which
is at a suitable level.

As a subdivision of this category, let us further divide the subject into
LIVING LANGUAGES and DEAD LANGUAGES.

A)   LIVING LANGUAGES

    i)   *YOU WILL ALMOST CERTAINLY HAVE BEEN DIRECTED TO NEWSPAPERS,
*      *MAGAZINES AND SO ON*, by your teacher.  If you have not explored
      this avenue, then do so.  A good library will either have them or
      can get them for you.

      *YOU CAN MAKE LIFE A LITTLE EASIER FOR YOURSELF, BY GETTING
      MAGAZINES ON SUBJECTS THAT INTEREST YOU.*  The most commonly
      available French magazines are on fashion - a subject that
      many find totally uninteresting.  So if you are interested in
      mountain-climbing, body-building, ballet, or whatever, try to
      get magazines and articles on those subjects.

    ii)   And don't let your material be lost.  *START A FILE ON SUBJECTS
      THAT INTEREST YOU.*  Add to the file regularly.  And don't worry
      that you can only read one word in ten.  If you are interested
      in the subject, you will find that your natural curiosity will
      force you to learn at least some of the unknown words.

      You will find that if you keep returning to your file, trying to
      make a little more sense of it each time, that very quickly you
      can read virtually everything.

      This idea of returning to the SAME FILE is not new to you.
      Almost certainly that is how you learned to read as a child.
      All of us had a couple of favourite books to which we returned
      again and again until we could recognise each word on every
      page.  If at the same time our parents read the words aloud, we
      learned to associate the sound and the word.

      Try it.  You'll find that the same approach works for a foreign
      language.

   iii)   *THERE IS ANOTHER SOURCE OF READING MATERIAL WHICH IS OFTEN
      OVERLOOKED :  THE TECHNICAL MANUALS.*

      You may be interested in computers.  You may read everything that
      is written on the subject.  You may know all the jargon and
      technical terms.  Well then, why not read it in FRENCH or RUSSIAN
      or SPANISH.  These manuals are ideal for your purpose.  Half of
      the words at least, you will recognise because they either look
      or sound like their English equivalents.

    iv)   Or, you can try to get textbooks written on your favourite subject
      in the language of your choice.  What does Pythagoras' theorem
      look like in Italian?  What does Macbeth sound like in French?
      And since you may already know what Pythagoras' theorem states,
      you know, roughly, what the Italian words stand for.

B)    DEAD LANGUAGES

    i)    In a dead language you are certainly hampered by lack of material.
         There are textbooks of course, but you won't find a ballet book
         in Latin.  And unless you are engrossed by Caesar's Wars or
         Roman politics, the standard texts are not uplifting.

         However, many authors have tried to correct this, and while you
         won't get the volume of material in Latin or Classical Greek,
         there are some books available.

    ii)   There are other methods available.  If you are at all imaginative
         you could try writing jokes to your friends in the language.  If
         they can respond, then you will develop your reading and writing
         skills at the same time.  Or you could cut out cartoons from the
         paper and translate the punch line into Latin or Greek or
         whatever.

         If you are good enough, you could even have your collection
         published.  There IS a need for such material after all.

3)    HOW TO WRITE A LANGUAGE

To write in a foreign language requires two basic notions :

a)    You must have at least a small vocabulary, and

b)    You must have some idea of how to put words together - i.e. the grammar
     of the language.

    i)    In a 'structured' course you are given a set of words to learn and a
         set of exercises to read.  Later you are given a set of sentences to
         translate into the language.

         Historically, this method of teaching was taken from mathematics.
         Even today, mathematics is still taught in this manner. In the meantime
         language teaching has adopted many new and exciting methods.  (Perhaps
         it's time for mathematics to learn from the languages.)

    ii)   In learning how to write a language, language teachers have found that
         by 'structuring' the teaching, they structure the student.  And in
         WRITING a language, that is the last thing you want.

         For instance, learning how to say :

         *"The pen of your aunt is in the garden."*

         is all very well.  And if that is the type of sentence that you wish to
         write then it is probably a good thing to know.

         But learning how to write :

         *"The astronaut entered the cabin of the space shuttle."*

         will force you to learn the same grammar and may have slightly more
         appeal.

iii)    Remember that one basic idea in studying (or writing) in a foreign
        language, is that *THE EXAMPLES SHOULD INTEREST YOU.*

        So the rule for writing is similar to that for reading :  *WRITE ABOUT
        THINGS THAT INTEREST YOU!!*

        Now while you may enjoy writing about fuel consumption in motorcycles,
        you must find out if what you are writing is intelligible.  When you do
        this, your procedure is very similar to the MISTAKES method described
        in the section on mathematics and science.

        In fact, in any subject where you must learn from your past mistakes,
        your procedure should be the same as set out in that chapter.

iv)     Thus, you will need a book in which to write your mistakes, a book to
        record new words - adding pictures is a good idea in languages, and
        some sort of daily diary to record your progress.

v)      But to improve your writing, YOU MUST WRITE!!

        Write to the President of France, to the Russian Ambassador, to any
        foreign speaking person you can think of.  If they reply, you have
        actually COMMUNICATED with someone in their own language.

        And isn't that what it is all about?

4)   HOW TO LISTEN TO A LANGUAGE

     "Much easier said than done" is the usual reaction to the idea of listening
     to someone in a foreign language.

     And, depending on what resources you have available, it may be very difficult
     indeed.

     On the other hand, there are many resources catering for the language student :

     i)     Can you find a language laboratory?

            For listening skills this is the best resource there is.  Your school
            may have one, the local library may have one, sometimes even private
            citizens have one.

     ii)    Can you buy your own language laboratory?

            Essentially, all you'd need would be a tape-recorder.  Cassettes
            designed for this purpose are commercially available.

     iii)   Can you get hold of pop records in the language of your choice?

            These will sometimes have the words printed on the cover.

     iv)    Or maybe you can find a reading of Macbeth in French.  The record
            certainly exists.

     v)     Can you get a friend who speaks the language fluently, to make up a
            tape for you.  What goes on the tape is up to you, but you may like to
            use the following idea which I have seen used successfully :

Ask your friend to record the same passage THREE times.  The first time, the passage should be read very slowly.  The next time, it should be read at half-pace.  The last time it should be read at full-speed as in conversation.

The effect is excellent for learning how to listen.  The first time through gives you time to get an idea of what is being said.  The second time through, you should be almost but not quite able to follow the speech.  The third time through will be almost unintelligible to you, since the speech will now be slurred, the pauses between the words will be missing and so on.  But now replay the entire three readings and you will find that your understanding will jump remarkably.  Repeat until you are satisfied that you have mastered what is being said at any of the speeds.

Then your friend must supply you with another tape.  Obviously, such friends are hard to come by, but perhaps you can work a trade-off; you'll teach them how to study in return for the tapes.

vi)   Does your T.V. cater for foreign films or is there a local cinema that shows foreign films.  (If you don't know then check your telephone directory.)

vii)  Are there local language groups?  Again, by checking your telephone directory, you may find that there is, say, a Classical Greek Society that you can join.

## 5)   HOW TO SPEAK A LANGUAGE

As with all other parts of language learning, you can only learn to speak by actually doing it.

While it may be possible to find a friend to read passages at different speeds onto a tape for you, it is much more difficult to find someone willing to listen to you talking about the pen of your aunt.

i)    Obviously you will have a chance to speak in the classroom, but you will need far more practice than this allows you.

If you have access to a language laboratory, or tapes of some sort or other, you should use them.  But these will only help you with pronunciation of individual words.  To SPEAK a language, you need to be able to hold conversations in it.  This means that you must find somewhere where the language is spoken freely.  Either that or CREATE such a place yourself.

ii)   In Chapter Eleven you will learn about 'study cells'.  A study cell is a group of people who get together for study purposes.  Such a cell would be ideal for studying languages.  If you don't have transport it is sometimes difficult to get together, but often your family will be prepared to help.  Perhaps you could set a night aside to have dinner together at one of your houses, where everything that is said must be in the language you are studying.

Or you could go to an Italian restaurant (if you are learning Italian, of course) and speak only Italian.

iii) There may be persons that you already know that would welcome con-
versation - however poor - with you.  Remember it is the people of
English speaking countries who generally speak only one language. Most
Europeans speak at least two.  So if you know anyone from Europe, it
is more than likely that you know a living language laboratory.
There is none better.

6)     AS WELL AS ....

In studying langauges, don't forget that you already know a lot about the
general principles of organisation, memory, recall of information, and so on.

For instance, the MISTAKES notion of Chapter Seven and the concentration
techniques of Chapter Four can be used here without change.  If you have not
read the chapter on mathematics and science because you are not studying them,
now is the time to do so.  The techniques described there are precisely what
you need in order to study languages - and vice versa of course!!

# CHAPTER TEN

## HOW TO SURVIVE THAT IMPORTANT EXAM

### SUMMARY

1....CHECK THE PAST PAPERS FOR FORMAT

2....FIND THE REGULARLY-ASKED QUESTIONS

3....LIST THE SELDOM-ASKED QUESTIONS

4....AS AN EMERGENCY

5....MAKE A REVISION TIMETABLE

6....RE-READ YOUR STUDY NOTES

7....PRACTICE DOING EXAMINATION QUESTIONS

8....WHAT NOT TO DO

9....WHAT TO DO THE NIGHT BEFORE THE EXAM

10...WHAT TO DO IN THE EXAM

11...WHAT TO DO AFTER THE EXAM

This section is devoted to students who have been following the Golden Rule, TREASURE YOUR MISTAKES, all year, (see Chapter Seven), and to those who have 'left it too late'.

It is assumed that you have read all the preceding sections.

There are several things that will be troubling you as the exam draws near. The one that should most concern you is ANXIETY.

All students to a greater or lesser degree, worry as time runs out. So what to do ....

### 1)   CHECK PAST PAPERS FOR FORMAT

The first thing is to find out all you can about the format of the exam; how many questions there are, what each one is worth, exactly what topics are to be tested, and so on.

In a class test you would find out all these things from your teacher. If, however, you are sitting for a public exam, you are much luckier : past papers are published and can be bought. Hence, your first task is to buy them - as many as possible.

Let's assume that you have a stack of past papers. You now have the problem of what to do with them. Remember that time is running out.

i)   *YOUR FIRST TASK IS TO CHECK THE FORMAT OF THE PAST PAPERS.* What is each question worth and so on - starting with the most recent paper and working backwards. (This is in case the format and marking scheme has changed.)

ii)  *NEXT, YOU MUST CHECK THROUGH THE PAPERS LOOKING FOR QUESTIONS THAT ALWAYS APPEAR.*

*For instance, if you are sitting for a calculus exam, your teacher MAY have stressed Simpson's Rule. However, on checking through the past papers, you may find that Simpson's Rule has been examined once in the last six years. Of course, this year may be the year it is asked again, but it is more likely that your teacher likes Simpson's Rule and therefore teaches it. This may be quite proper DURING THE YEAR, but not just before an exam.*

Of course, while you will find a lot of questions that are asked regularly, and also a lot of questions that are asked very seldom, most of the papers will be made up of in-between questions. And while it is relatively easy to prepare for regularly-asked questions, and it is exceptionally easy to prepare for seldom-asked questions, preparing for the in-betweens is 'murder'.

2)   THE REGULARLY-ASKED QUESTION

To prepare for these you should be able to do ONE OF THEM - and then check that all the others are of a similar nature. (I'm assuming you don't have time to do more.)

If you find any hints for yourself, write them down as you find them - many students remember the last thing they wrote down the night before the exam, and it can mean the difference between pass or fail.

If you have the time, speak to your teacher about what you believe to be the case about the regularly-asked question - perhaps he or she can add something to your knowledge. Friends may also shed light on these questions. The point is, that everyone will have found out something about these questions, so ask as many people as possible.

3)   THE SELDOM-ASKED QUESTION

Here your problem is quite different. You must decide whether it is at all likely that this question will be asked. If you decide that the likelihood is small, then it may be worth your while to leave it out of your schedule altogether, and chance it.

The big question you must ask yourself is ;  Could the time I spend learning this question be better spent, (i.e. would it get me more marks) on another topic? Your teacher must be asked this question, but ultimately you must decide.

4)   AS AN EMERGENCY

Past papers are generally made up of questions that are in-between in frequency. If you have done very little work throughout the year, then there is not much that can be done a week or so before an exam. If you are in this unhappy circumstance, you must pick a friend that HAS done some work and take his or her advice.

Teachers will also help with 'emergency' work, but it goes against a teacher's grain not to give the background, the history, the significance, and so on of what they teach. You may find therefore, that teachers give rather more than you ask - which wastes even more of your time. However, teachers can give insights into what to study much better than friends, if you can get it out of them - especially on in-between questions.

*So, for instance, if you are sitting for an exam which is based on calculus, then an in-betwen question that will generally occur four or five times PER EXAM, is the question of solving inequalities, both linear and quadratic. Now, not too many students will be able to tell you this, but any teacher could. And a question that occurs four or five times, may be worth anything up to 25%!!*

In a mathematics or science exam, you will generally find help by reading the worked examples in your textbook. Many students never read texts, but just use them for exercises. Now is the time to change.

But apart from these few hints, it is very difficult to help.

5)   MAKE A REVISION TIMETABLE

Since homework may have ceased altogether, or at least been diminished, your timetable must be changed.

Use the same principles in drawing up your revision timetable as you did in drawing up the original. Remember to :

i)    *BE PRECISE*

ii)   *KEEP A BALANCE BETWEEN SUBJECTS*

iii)  *STUDY THE HARDEST SUBJECTS FIRST*

iv)   *ALLOCATE TIME IN PROPORTION TO THE VALUE OF THE TOPIC IN TERMS OF MARKS*

v)    *REMEMBER YOUR HEALTH AND RECREATION*

6)   RE-READ YOUR STUDY NOTES, GOING OVER KEY POINTS, CHECKING THAT YOU REMEMBER LISTS OF KEY POINTS, ETC.

Keep your textbooks by you as reference.

7)   GIVE YOURSELF PRACTICE IN ANSWERING EXAM QUESTIONS

You may find that by checking the format of past papers, that you will be required to write six essays in two hours.

This means twenty minutes per essay.

If you take thirty minutes to write a similar essay, you have a problem. You may :

i)    Write too slowly - learn to 'speed-write', but remember to make it legible.

ii)   Write too much - perhaps your teacher can help you here. Either way, check to see that you are sticking to the point.

iii)   Not know your lists of key points well enough and are hence wasting valuable time  trying to remember them.

iv)    Not be planning your essay in advance.

Any or all of the above can be fixed.  But constant practice in doing exam questions under exam conditions is the way to mark your progress.

8)   WHAT NOT TO DO

i)     DON'T spend more time on a topic than that topic is worth.

ii)    DON'T be led astray by enthusiastic friends - or teachers - into studying their favourite topic.

iii)   DON'T try to do every question in the textbook or every question in the past papers on the night before the exam.

iv)    DON'T forget that you had a lot of common sense before you went to school and were influenced by 'educators'.  Use this common sense.

v)     DON'T expect miracles and don't lose your head.  (Many students discover a lot of knowledge for themselves in exams.)

9)   WHAT TO DO ON THE NIGHT BEFORE THE EXAM

If you have been following the methods outlined in this book, your night before will consist of quiet revision of facts, formulae and mistakes.  The hard work will have been done during the course, and you will have been consciously preparing for this night.

Even so, there are a few points to note :

i)     *MAKE SURE YOU GET AN AMPLE NIGHT'S SLEEP.*  Having a clear head will be worth more to you than cramming a few more facts in.  Especially if it means a headache on the next day.

ii)    *DON'T MISTAKE THE DATE, TIME AND PLACE OF AN EXAMINATION.*  You would be surprised at how common it is for a student to miss an exam altogether.  Remember too, to take with you all necessary materials - your examination number, your calculator, with spare batteries, pens, pencils, paint brushes, etc.

iii)   *AVOID LENGTHY CONVERSATIONS WITH OTHER STUDENTS IMMEDIATELY BEFORE AN EXAM.*  You may hear that someone else has studied both X and Y, whereas you have only studied X.  This may sap your self-confidence, which is the last thing you want.  Let's face it :  it is now too late to do anything about it.

10)  WHAT TO DO IN THE EXAM

Always listen to the instructions that will be given to you by the supervisor.  Once you are allowed to commence, then :

i)     *READ THE PAPER ALL THE WAY THROUGH.*  Mark which questions that you MUST do, and those where you have to make a choice.  Take your time doing this, it is time well spent.

ii)   As you read the paper, *NOTE ANY THOUGHTS THAT WILL HELP YOU ANSWER THE QUESTION.*

iii)  *PLAN YOUR TIME.*   If all questions are of equal value then divide your time equally.  If not, then allocate your time proportionally.  It is best to try to leave ten minutes at the end of the paper for emergencies.

iv)   *ANSWER THE EASY QUESTIONS FIRST.*  In this way you are sure of maximising your marks.  Remember that there is no question that EVERYONE will find easy.  The ones YOU find easy will stop many other candidates.

v)    *WATCH THE WORDING OF THE QUESTION.*  'Explain' will mean something different to 'Discuss' for instance.  Make sure you answer the question.  A very common mistake is for a student to write an excellent essay but to get no marks for it since it answered a different question than the one asked.

vi)   *PLAN YOUR ANSWER.*  Jot down an outline of the format of what you intend to say at the start of the question.  Try to follow a logical structure in your answer and above all, remember the Golden Rule for writing essays :

      STICK TO THE POINT

vii)  *IF YOU GET 'BOGGED DOWN' IN A QUESTION, LEAVE IT.*  If you have planned your time correctly, you will be able to come back to it later.  Even if you can't come back, you will earn marks by doing other questions instead.

viii) *BE CAREFUL TO WATCH YOUR TIME.*  Many people lose track of the time while answering their favourite question.  You will usually get a better result by answering ALL the questions that you have to, (even if you can't spend all the time on them that you would wish), rather than write perfectly on only a few questions.  Work on the assumption that in any essay question, the first 10 out of say 15 marks are relatively easy to earn.  The last 5 are going to be very difficult to earn.

ix)   *DON'T LEAVE EARLY.*  You can always refine an answer, or check the working of a problem, or get a last minute inspiration while in the exam room.  Leave it and you can't.

x)    *IF TIME IS RUNNING OUT, THEN GIVE OUTLINES OF YOUR ANSWERS.*  These are best given in point form.  You can even give outlines in mathematics and science exams and expect marks for them.  *ALWAYS COMPARE YOURSELF WITH THE PERSON WHO LEAVES THE QUESTION BLANK OR WHO LEAVES THE EXAM ROOM ALTOGETHER.*

## 11)  WHAT TO DO AFTER THE EXAM

This is normally the period of regret.  Some students are so affected by what they think is a poor performance in one exam, that they cannot perform in the next day's exam.

Quite often too, the supposed bad performance turns out to be not so bad after all.

But I am not concerned with that,  Having read this book you should know
I would expect you to look at the exam - and its result - as another
experience to learn from.

i)    *Whatever the result, YOU CAN GAIN PERSONAL INSIGHT into how you
      function under this sort of pressure.*

ii)   *YOU CAN LEARN WHAT AREAS OF KNOWLEDGE are your weaknesses and which
      are your strengths.*

iii)  *YOU CAN LEARN WHETHER YOUR KNOWLEDGE GAINING METHODS and study
      methods are adequate for this sort of exam.*

iv)   *YOU CAN LEARN MUCH MORE FROM THE EXAM and what you did in preparation.
      But to do so you must accept it for what it is :  another experience
      that you can learn from.*

If you let it dominate your life and behaviour then you have forgotten the
point :

THERE IS LIFE AFTER SCHOOL - AND YOU NEED TO KNOW HOW TO FIND
OUT THE KNOWLEDGE THAT INTERESTS YOU NO MATTER WHERE YOU ARE.
THE TECHNIQUES IN THIS BOOK CAN BE APPLIED ANYWHERE AT ANY TIME.

# CHAPTER ELEVEN

## HOW TO STUDY AS A PRIVATE STUDENT OR AT UNIVERSITY

SUMMARY

1....THE GENERAL PROBLEM

2....STUDY CELLS

3....NOTICE BOARDS

4....HIRING TEACHERS

5....ALTERNATIVES TO TEACHER

6....THE LIBRARY

7....LEARNING BY COMPUTER

Again I am assuming that you have read the preceding sections. The idea of learning from your mistakes and hence not being afraid of them, is basic to all productive learning.

1)   THE GENERAL PROBLEM

    i)   The problems faced by the private student are similar to those of the university or college student. Neither one has a ready made system in which the student can meet other students doing the same courses. Hence there is great difficulty in finding someone with whom to just TALK ABOUT YOUR PROBLEMS.

        Anyone who has been in this situation, will laugh at the 'problems' faced by students at school. There you may have thirty other students doing the same course as yourself and maybe half a dozen teachers who can help you within calling distance.

        If the private student could overcome this one problem, most of the other problems would sort themselves out. It is possible, but it generally takes some imagination.

        The other main problem faced by these students is a management of time. As a private student, you may be at work for ten hours a day, raising a family or have social comitments. Finding time to study is almost impossible. The study timetable mentioned in Chapter Two must be set up and worked to as much as possible.

    ii)   If as a private student you are doing any of the sciences, psychology, statistics or computer science, you will have laboratory classes to attend as well as theory classes. Each hour spent in a laboratory may mean another hour writing up the experiment. Thus two hours are NOT AVAILABLE for study purposes.

        For those of you who have not worked under these conditions I should mention that time spent in the lab means time you can't spend writing up experiments, digesting results, thinking, studying, doing the washing, preparing meals, and so on.

2)     THE STUDY CELL

A common strategy among students who are older or more mature than schools allow, is to form 'study cells'. A study cell comprises several students studying the same course who group together for interchange of ideas. Many students need this support for a reason unknown to most school students : they are often working long hours  and simply don't have the time to study the  entire course. Thus, in the study cell, each student may study a different part of the course and teaches it to the rest of the cell. The problem is to organise the study cell to begin with ....

3)     THE NOTICE BOARD

i)     If you are attached to a tertiary college, a notice on the major - and minor - notice boards that you are doing such-and-such a course and would like to form a study cell with other students doing the same course, may bring results. (Sometimes it brings surprising results, so be careful in giving name, sex, and so on.)

ii)     Or if you have access to a computer bulletin  board, you may be able to contact other students doing your course. The computer bulletin board is ideal if you are not attached to a tertiary college, but just intend to sit for some public examination by yourself. If computer bulletin  boards are unavailable, advertisements in local papers or over local radio are cheap and reach a large audience. Again take precautions and don't give name, address, etc.

4)     HIRING TEACHERS

If you can form a study cell, you may consider the idea of hiring a teacher! I mention this because to many people, 'teachers work in schools'. Not so, obviously. Teachers will teach anywhere and are not expensive when hired by a group.

If you are unable to form a cell and can find no-one, I sympathise. All I can suggest is that you approach the local school and see if a teacher can help you there. While some teachers will not countenance such a thing, others will be only too grateful that an older student has asked for help.

5)     ALTERNATIVES TO TEACHERS

There are many other ways you can gain access to teachers.

i)     Correspondence Schools often have courses designed for students who don't have access to institutions such as colleges and schools. If not you will always find them helpful in any matters affecting private students.

ii)     Some Education Departments have Colleges of External Studies attached to them. So too do many universities.

To get in contact with such organisation, check your telephone book.

6)     THE LIBRARY

While the library has an important function at a school, its importance is overwhelming to the private or university student.

It is imperative that you know at least, what is available at a library, and preferably, how to find what you want for yourself.

Libraries hold education days to show members how to use the many facilities that are available.  With the increasing use of the computer, a working knowledge of how to get the library's computer to work for you is mandatory. Science students in particular, make life very difficult for themselves by not knowing how to operate library equipment.

7)    LEARNING BY COMPUTER

As well as using computers in libraries, many companies make entire courses available to persons who own their own computer.

There are two ways you can do this :

i)    You can buy the entire course on a set of floppy disks which you can then run on your own machine.

ii)   Or, if you own a modem, you can join a computer database which specialises in education courses, and have the course sent over the telephone wires to your computer.

These courses are written specifically for students AT ALL LEVELS.  Some will even prepare you for specific exams.  Their cost need not be great - after the initial cost of the computer - and you should certainly investigate them.

*Private students and university students have a terribly hard life.  If you know any, be kind to them.*

# CHAPTER TWELVE

# HOW TO BE A PARENT

## SUMMARY

1....THE GOLDEN TRIAD

2....DON'T CLAIM THAT YOU DON'T UNDERSTAND THE WORK

3....DON'T LECTURE

4....EDUCATION HAS NOT BECOME EASIER

5....BY BEING OLDER, YOU DO HAVE VALUABLE HELP TO GIVE

6....LEARN TO LISTEN

7....PLATITUDES HELP NO-ONE

8....TRY FAMILY MEETINGS

9....READ THIS BOOK

10...RELAX

This section is devoted to parents of students.  It will be short.

i)    As the supporter of your student you supply food, shelter, and money.  MANY PARENTS THEREFORE SEE THEMSELVES AS INVESTING IN THEIR STUDENT'S FUTURE. And knowing the value of money, many parents look for a return on their investment.

That's where the trouble starts :

Because your student does NOT see himself or herself as an investment. Students prefer to think of themselves as people!!!

The friction between parents and students may be of this nature.

ii)   OR IT MAY BE THAT YOU HAVE OTHER UNREALISTIC GOALS FOR YOUR STUDENT.  You may wish that he or she should not make the same mistakes that you did.

iii)  OR IT MAY BE THAT YOUR STUDENT HAS UNREALISTIC GOALS.  He or she may wish to do X when you know from bitter experience that X will only lead to heart-break.

iv)   OR IT MAY BE THAT THE STUDENT'S PEERS EXPECT A CERTAIN RESULT WHEN YOU, AS A PARENT, EXPECT SOMETHING ENTIRELY DIFFERENT.

Is there a way out of these problems?

Well there is no easy way but a few suggestions are in order.

1)    THE GOLDEN TRIAD

Supporting a student means more than physical and materialistic support.  At
some stage you will have used the GOLDEN TRIAD :

> *THE SMILE OF ENCOURAGEMENT*
>
> *THE APPRECIATIVE WORD*
>
> *THE HUG*

If the last time you used them was when your student was a baby, try them
again now.  They worked when your student was trying to walk and talk, and
you'll find that they still work now.  No one is so old that the GOLDEN
TRIAD won't make him or her feel 10 feet tall.

2)    DON'T CLAIM THAT YOU DON'T UNDERSTAND THEIR WORK

That is just avoiding your responsibility.  Simply by reading this book you
are in a position to offer invaluable advice on organisation, study methods
and so on.

3)    DON'T LECTURE

It may be true that '*In your day* ... ' but your student needs help not
moralising.

4)    EDUCATION HAS NOT BECOME EASIER

Even if courses had the same content as twenty years ago - they don't, they
have much more - there are so many more people trying for that job or that
place in college or university, that today's student must work much, much
harder and score many more marks than you did.

5)    BY BEING OLDER YOU DO HAVE VALUABLE HELP TO GIVE

You know how to organise things to aid in the student's work, a family trip
to a museum for science, or just an outing for relaxation.  You may have
friends that can help on specific topics or subjects where you cannot.  You
can organise time - something which school students can seldom do.  More than
anything, you can take a positive interest in your student WITHOUT trying to
take over.  Ask your student if he or she would like help.  Offer to hear
the French 'vocab' or the science formulae.  Ask questions about what
happens in school and listen to the answers.  *Remember it is the student
whose home life is aligned with the school life that has the edge on the
others.*

6)    LEARN TO LISTEN

Often a sympathetic ear is all that is needed.  By giving advice you may
think you are helping - and you may be.  But think of your own reaction
when someone gives unasked-for advice.  And sometimes, even when you ask
for advice, you only want the other person to listen.  Listen to your student
very carefully before giving advice.  Most of the time the problem will
vanish as he or she talks to you.

## 7) PLATITUDES DON'T HELP

So never say that *'Science is terribly important these days'* or *'Never put off till tomorrow ...'*

You may believe it to be true. But just try to recall the monumental problems that you faced as a teenager. The pressures put on students by their peers may cause them to be terrified of going to school. If they tell you that they don't want to go to school and you reply that *'Knowledge is no burden to carry'*, can you really blame parent-bashers? Try to look behind the problem. Usually you will find another problem that may be fixed. Then the original problem will vanish.

## 8) TRY FAMILY MEETINGS

Family meetings should be held weekly, on a night when everyone is home.

They can serve many purposes, but can only be successful if *EVERYONE IS GIVEN A HEARING.*

Students don't wish an absence of rules but you will find that rules are far less likely to be broken by people who had a hand in their formation.

Thus, on the schooling side, you can use family meetings to :

i)   *DISCUSS COMING EVENTS THAT AFFECT THE USUAL ROUTINE OF THE FAMILY.* If you know a week in advance that a Rock Concert is a necessity for your student's well-being, you may be able to plan around it. You may be able to help rearrange the study timetable so that no time is lost by going to the concert.

Once your student realises that you are prepared to listen, understand and help with their problems, you may be surprised at the result - pleasantly, I hope.

ii)  *YOU CAN LAY THE GROUND RULES FOR THE COMING YEAR.* These must be seen to be fair. You should decide how much time you expect your student to spend at the desk each night. Decide what to do in the case of unexpected breaks in the routine - your favourite aunt arrives without notice to stay for a few days, and so on.

iii) *THE FAMILY MEETING IS A GOOD PLACE TO AIR YOUR OWN GRIEVANCES - BUT YOU MUST EXPECT TO HEAR YOUR FAMILY'S GRIEVANCES AS WELL.* On top of this, you must try to find solutions for grievances. Ask for help. Listen to suggestions. And act on them.

The meeting is the ideal way of getting closer to your family. It may not work the first few times. But if your student/students see that their suggestions are being listened to, they will respond accordingly.

## 9) READ THIS BOOK

If you have turned to this page because it was 'the only part that affected you', then you should now go back and read the lot.

i)   *YOUR STUDENT WILL NEED HELP TO SET UP SOME OF THE SYSTEMS MENTIONED HERE* - you can help!

ii)   *YOUR STUDENT NEEDS AN ENVIRONMENT THAT WILL PROMOTE GOOD STUDY HABITS* - you can help!

iii)  *YOUR STUDENT WILL NEED TO BE PROTECTED FROM DISTRACTIONS* - you can help!

iv)   *YOUR STUDENT NEEDS ALL THE SUPPORT THAT YOU AS A PARENT CAN GIVE* - you can help!

## 10)  RELAX

Of all, this is the hardest and the most successful.  If you can learn from your own mistakes as a parent, you will find that you can adjust to the problems of having a student in the family with great ease.

If you are prepared to try, you'll find that students are very exciting persons to have around.  Among other things, they give new insights into all the common, everyday things that we take for granted.

## CHAPTER THIRTEEN

## HOW TO BE A TEACHER

AS TEACHERS, WE OFTEN FORGET ONE THING :

WE WERE GOOD AT OUR SUBJECT!!

a)    This forgetfulness causes more grief among our students than anything else.
      We perceive that one style of teaching is not producing the results we
      demand, so we change to a different style, and maybe to a third.

      But no matter what system we try, we are bound to fail if we cannot realise
      that very few people respond to the 'normal' methods of teaching no matter
      what they be.

      For no matter what style of teaching we use, we are still under the
      influence of the concepts of 'right' and 'wrong'.  A student who answers
      a question will either get it right or wrong!!  It's obvious.  Ask anyone.
      Everything is based on it.

      *BUT IT IS NOT TRUE!!*

b)    Something else can happen as well.  The student who gets the question wrong,
      learns not only that his or her working is wrong but that he or she is not
      as capable as the student who got it right.

      *SO THAT A STUDENT WHO ANSWERS A QUESTION :*

      *1)     CAN GET IT RIGHT or CAN GET IT WRONG,*

      *but, no matter which*

      *2)     WILL LEARN THAT HE OR SHE IS BETTER OR WORSE THAN OTHER STUDENTS.*

      And hence, not only is the student's ABILITY being questioned, but also the
      student's SELF ESTEEM.

      And that of course is why WE liked our subject so much :  we could do it and
      hence our self esteem was sky high.

      But what about those who got the question wrong?  And the next question and
      the next?

      Their self esteem must have taken a battering.  Which would partially
      explain why so many people hate school with a vengeance!

c)    The point I would like to make is this :

      The 'right/wrong' method of teaching - or running a school - will harm more
      persons than it helps.  If a student has not learned how to cope with
      consistently getting questions wrong, then sooner or later he or she will
      start hating school, and probably other learning as well.

*THE ALTERNATE METHOD I WOULD PROPOSE IS THIS :*

*A STUDENT WHO DOES A QUESTION :*

1)     *CAN GET IT RIGHT or CAN GET IT WRONG,*

*but, no matter which*

2)     *LOOKS ON FAILURE AS AN INTRINSIC PART OF THE LEARNING PROCESS.*

d)   Now, such an approach demands many changes in behaviour on our behalf.   No longer can an exam serve to grade students - for as soon as a student realises that this is the case, then the idea of learning from mistakes goes out the window and we return to the previous model.

Nor can we use the ideas of *'if-you-don't-listen-to-me-you'll-fail'* or any form of punishment for failure.   For if the idea is to learn from your own mistakes, then you can hardly be punished for learning by making them.

Nor can you reward for 'success' at the expense of someone else who 'failed'.

e)   As you try to implement this method, you will find that you will take a much more scientific approach to teaching.   That is, you will view learning as something to be experimented with - where, as in science, a negative result can be just as significant as a positive one.   This attitude, if transmitted to your students, will remove much of the fear and anxiety they experience.

The lack of fear and anxiety, may lead to students who will readily respond: "*I don't know - why don't we try such and such?*" With patience and persistence they may find that through such an approach, they can discover and invent their own learning.

WHATEVER THEY DISCOVER MUST BE BETTER THAN THE 'I-HATE-SCHOOL' PRODUCTS OF YESTERDAY.

# GLOSSARY

# Algebra

## Mistake

Solve $3(x + 4) = x$

$$3x + 12 = x$$
$$3x = x - 12$$
$$x = \frac{x - 12}{3}$$

You can't end up with x's on both sides

Simplify $-2(x-3)$
$$-2x - 6$$

Simplify $2(x-3)-(4-x)$
$$2x - 3 - 4 - x$$
$$x - 1$$

3 mistakes
1) $2(x-3) = 2x - 6$
2) $-(4-x) = -1(4-x)$
$$= -4 + x$$
3) $-3 - 4 = -7$

## Correction

$$3(x + 4) = x$$
$$3x + 12 = x$$
$$3x + 12 - x = 0$$
$$2x + 12 = 0$$
$$2x = -12$$
$$x = -6$$

Always get the unknowns on one side.

$$-2(x-3)$$
$$-2x + 6$$

Two negatives make a positive

$$2(x-3)-1(4-x)$$
$$2x - 6 - 4 + x$$
$$3x - 10$$

If you put the -1 before the brackets you can expand them easier

LIST 1 : This is a page from the mistake book of a Year 8 student. Here the student is just *listing* mistakes, so that he can diagnose any weaknesses in his work.

70

$$\sqrt{a^2+b^2}$$

You can't simplify this!
Don't confuse with:

$$\sqrt{(a+b)^2} = a+b$$

<u>March</u> Question:
    Solve for $x$:       $x^2 = 4p^2 + 8q^2$
    Solution:         $x^2 = 4(p^2 + 2q^2)$
                      $x = \pm 2\sqrt{p^2 + 2q^2}$

I wrote: —————————————— $x = 2p + 2.8284q$

<u>March</u> (same test)
    Question: Find $x$.

Solution:
    $y^2 = x^2 + z^2$, 
              Pythagoras
    $x^2 = y^2 - z^2$
    $x = \sqrt{y^2 - z^2}, \quad x > 0$

(You put $x>0$ because you should really put a $\pm$ sign except since its a triangle the sides must be positive.)

I wrote: $x = y - z$

<u>June</u> Question: Simplify $\sqrt{a^2 + b^2 + 2ab}$
Solution: $\sqrt{a^2 + b^2 + 2ab} = \sqrt{(a+b)^2}$
                             $= a+b$

I wrote: $a + b + \sqrt{2ab}$

LIST 2 :  Here the student has found that a particular mistake is occurring
            many times and must be fixed.  She has thus formed a *category* of
            mistakes.  The number of categories will depend on what mistakes
            you make.

Quotient Rule

$$\frac{d}{dx}\left(\frac{u}{v}\right) = \frac{vu' - uv'}{v^2}$$

Standard Question 1.

Differentiate $\dfrac{e^x}{x^2-x}$

solution:

Let $y = \dfrac{e^x}{x^2-x}$

$$\therefore \frac{dy}{dx} = \frac{(x^2-x)e^x - e^x(2x-1)}{(x^2-x)^2}$$

$$= \frac{e^x(x^2-x-2x+1)}{(x^2-x)^2}$$

$$= \frac{e^x(x^2-3x+1)}{(x^2-x)^2}$$

I used to differentiate the top and the bottom — you **never** do this)

You should go as far as possible. Normally you'd be finding the max or min. of something and you'd have to equate $\dfrac{dy}{dx}$ to 0 + then you'd need it as simple as possible.

Q2. Find the maximum value of $\dfrac{x}{e^x}$

solution    Let $y = \dfrac{x}{e^x}$

$$\therefore \frac{dy}{dx} = \frac{e^x \cdot 1 - x \cdot e^x}{(e^x)^2} = \frac{e^x(1-x)}{(e^x)^2}$$

$$= 0 \text{ for stat. pt.}$$

$$\therefore x = 1, \quad e^x \neq 0$$

Test $x=1$

when $x = 1^-$, $\dfrac{dy}{dx} > 0$     when $x = 1^+$, $\dfrac{dy}{dx} < 0$

$+ \diagup ^{\circ} \diagdown -$   $\therefore$ there is a maximum at $x = 1$.

LIST 3 :   Here the student has used a standard question and an earlier mistake to *illustrate* a topic.

## SAMPLE STUDY/HOMEWORK TIMETABLE 1 - JUNIOR (YEAR 9, 10)

| TIME | MONDAY | TUESDAY | WEDNESDAY | THURSDAY | FRIDAY |
|---|---|---|---|---|---|
| A.M. 7.00 - 7.25 | Rise, prepare for school, etc. | | | | |
| 7.30 - 8.00 Memory Subjects Study | English, Topic ...... | History, Topic ...... | Commerce, Topic ...... | Language, Topic ...... | Science, Topic ...... |
| 8.05 - 4.55 P.M. | School day activities | | | | |
| 5.00 - 5.25 | Homework set at school | | | | |
| 5.30 - 5.55 | Homework set at school | | | | |
| 6.00 - 6.25 | Meal, relaxation, T.V. | | | | |
| 6.30 - 6.55 | Meal, relaxation, T.V. | | | | |
| 7.00 - 7.25 | Homework set at school | | | | |
| 7.30 - 7.55 | Homework set at school | | | | |
| 8.00 - 8.25 Study Times | Language, Topic ...... | Commerce, Topic ...... | English, Topic ...... | History, Topic ...... | English, Topic ...... |
| 8.30 - 8.55 Study Times | Maths, Topic ...... | Science, Topic ...... | Maths, Topic ...... | Science, Topic ...... | Maths, Topic ...... |
| 9.00 - 9.55 | Relaxation - bed by 10.00 p.m. | | | | |

| TIME | SATURDAY |
|---|---|
| A.M. 8.00 - 8.25 | Rise, dress |
| 8.30 - 8.55 | Breakfast |
| 9.00 - 9.25 | History, Topic ...... |
| 9.30 - 9.55 (Study time) | Commerce, Topic ...... |
| 10.00 - 10.25 (Study time) | Language, Topic ...... |
| 10.30 - 10.55 | Relaxation |
| 11.00 - 11.25 | Preparation for next week |
| 11.30 - 11.55 | Preparation for next week |
| 12.00 - 12.25 Study Time | Weaker subjects |
| 12.30 - 12.55 | Relaxation, recreation, etc. |

NOTE : This is a junior year student studying English, History, Commerce, Language, Science, Mathematics.

# SAMPLE STUDY/HOMEWORK TIMETABLE 2 - SENIOR

| TIME | MONDAY | TUESDAY | WEDNESDAY | THURSDAY | FRIDAY |
|---|---|---|---|---|---|
| A.M. 6.30 - 7.00 | ← Rise, dress, etc. → | | | | |
| 7.00 - 7.25 | | | | | |
| 7.30 - 7.55 | ← Set homework → | | | | |
| 8.00 - / 4.30 P.M. | Breakfast, travel, lunch, school activities, afternoon snack, etc. | | | | |
| 4.30 - 4.55 | ← Set homework → | | | | |
| 5.00 - 5.25 | | | | | |
| 5.30 - 5.55 | ← Set homework → | | | | |
| 6.00 - 6.25 | | | | | |
| 6.30 - 7.00 | ← Tea/dinner break, T.V. → | | | | |
| 7.00 - 7.25 | | | | | |
| 7.30 - 7.55 | ← Set homework → | | | | |
| 8.00 - 8.25 | | | | | |
| 8.30 - 8.55 | Mod.Hist. Topic .... | Geography Topic .... | English Topic .... | Biology Topic .... | Mod.Hist. Topic .... |
| 9.00 - 9.25 (not homework times) | Maths Topic .... | French Topic .... | Maths Topic .... | French Topic .... | Maths Topic .... |
| 9.30 - 9.55 (not homework time) | English Topic .... | Biology Topic .... | Mod.Hist. Topic .... | Geography Topic .... | English Topic .... |
| 10.00 - 10.25 | ← Supper, relaxation, bed by 10.30 p.m. → | | | | |

| TIME | SATURDAY | SUNDAY |
|---|---|---|
| 7.30 - 8.00 | ← Rise, dress → | Preparation |
| 8.00 - 8.25 | Geography Topic .... | for next week |
| 8.30 - 8.55 (not homework times) | French Topic .... | |
| 9.00 - 9.25 | ← Breakfast → | |
| 9.30 - 9.55 (not homework time) | Biology Topic .... and | Reading |
| 10.00 - 10.25 | Set homework | re-reading set texts |
| 10.30 - 10.55 | Set homework | |
| 11.00 - 11.25 | ← Relaxation → | |
| 11.30 - 11.55 | Set homework | Further study |
| 12.00 - 12.25 | Set homework | in weaker subjects |
| 12.30 - 12.55 | Set homework | |
| 1.00 - | Lunch, recreation, etc. | Lunch, recreation, etc. |

NOTES : 1) This is a senior year student studying six equal time subjects - English, Modern History, Geography, Biology, French, Mathematics.
2) This student has no commitments apart from study.

## SAMPLE STUDY/HOMEWORK TIMETABLE 3 – SENIOR

| TIME | MONDAY | TUESDAY | WEDNESDAY | THURSDAY | FRIDAY |
|---|---|---|---|---|---|
| A.M. 7.00 – 7.25 | ←—— Rise, dress, etc. ——→ | | | | |
| 7.30 – 4.55 P.M. | ←—— School day activities ——→ | | | | |
| 5.00 – 5.50 | ←— Set homework —→ | | Sports Training | ←— Set homework —→ | |
| 6.00 – 6.50 | ←— Set homework —→ | | Travel to home, etc. | ←— Set homework —→ | |
| 7.00 – 7.50 | ←— Meal, relaxation —→ | | | | Study time |
| 8.00 – 8.50 | ←— Set homework —→ | | | | Chemistry |
| 9.00 – 9.50 | ←— Set homework —→ | | | | Maths |
| 10.00 – 11.00 Study time | English / Maths | Physics / Economics | Chemistry / Gen.Studies | English / Maths | Economics / Physics |
| 11.00 – 11.25 | ←—— Supper, Bed by 11.30 p.m. ——→ | | | | |

| TIME | SATURDAY | SUNDAY |
|---|---|---|
| A.M. 7.30 – 7.55 | ←—— Rise, dress, etc. ——→ | |
| 8.00 – 8.50 | ←—— Breakfast ——→ | |
| | Travel | Set homework |
| 9.00 – 9.50 | Saturday | Set homework |
| 10.00 – 10.50 | Morning | Set homework |
| 11.00 – 11.50 | Job / Chores | Church service |
| 12.00 – 12.50 | | – |
| 1.00 – 1.50 | Lunch / Travel | Lunch / Reading |
| 2.00 – 2.50 | Sports | and Re-reading Set texts |
| 3.00 – 3.50 | Match | Further study in weaker subjects |
| 4.00 – 4.50 | Sports | Relaxation break |
| 5.00 – 5.50 | – | Preparation for next week |

NOTES : 1) This is senior student studying six unequal time subjects – English, Mathematics, General Studies, Chemistry, Economics, and Physics.

2) The student has various commitments over the week – Sports training on Wednesday afternoon, Saturday morning job and chores, Saturday afternoon match, and Sunday church.

SAMPLE STUDY/HOMEWORK TIMETABLE 4 – SENIOR

| TIME | MONDAY | TUESDAY | WEDNESDAY | THURSDAY | FRIDAY | SATURDAY | SUNDAY |
|---|---|---|---|---|---|---|---|
| 6.30 – 7.30 a.m. | | | Revision | | | | |
| 7.30 – 9.00 | | Breakfast, travel time | | | | | |
| 9.00 a.m. –<br>12.00 –<br>3.30 p.m. | | | SCHOOL | | | Essays | Essays |
| 4.00 – 5.30 | Gym | Run | Gym | Squash | Gym | | |
| 5.30 – 6.30 | | Homework and Prep. | | | | | Essays |
| 6.30 – 7.30 | | Dinner and television | | | | | Essays |
| 7.30 – 8.30 | | Homework and Prep. | | | | | |
| 8.30 – 9.30 | Study English | Study Physics | Study Chemistry | Study English | Study Physics | | Prep. for next week |
| 9.30 – 10.30 | Study Maths | Study French | Study History | Study Maths | Study French | | |

NOTE : This is how a timetable may look if prepared at the *start of a year*, before the normal commitments appear.

SAMPLE STUDY/HOMEWORK TIMETABLE 5 - SENIOR

| TIME | MONDAY | TUESDAY | WEDNESDAY | THURSDAY | FRIDAY | SATURDAY | SUNDAY |
|---|---|---|---|---|---|---|---|
| 6.30 – 7.30 a.m. | Revision | Training | Revision | Homework + Prep. | Training | | |
| 7.30 – 8.30 | | Training | | | Training | | |
| 8.30 – 12.00 | | | | | | Sport | Essays |
| 12.00 – 2.00 p.m. | | | ← School → | | | Study Ind.Arts. | Squash |
| 2.00 – 3.00 | | | | | | Study Ind.Arts. | |
| 3.00 – 4.00 | | | | | | Study Music | |
| 4.00 – 5.30 | Gym | Homework + Prep. | Sport | Homework + Prep. | Homework + Prep. | | |
| 5.30 – 6.30 | Homework + Prep. | Homework + Prep. | Sport | Dinner | Homework + Prep. | | |
| 6.30 – 7.30 | Dinner + TV | Dinner + TV | Dinner | Homework + Prep. | Dinner + TV | | Essays |
| | | | Homework + Prep. | | | | |
| 7.30 – 8.30 | Homework + Prep. | Study Anc. History | Homework + Prep. | Sports club Meeting | Study Anc. History | | Essays |
| 8.30 – 9.30 | Study English | Study Art | Study Ind.Arts | Sports club Meeting | Study Art | | Prep. for next week |
| 9.30 – 10.30 | Study Maths | Relax/ Read | Study Music | Study English | | | |
| 10.30 – 11.30 | | | | Study Maths | | | |

NOTE : This is the sporting person's timetable. It contains the same homework, prep. and study time as the previous one (No. 4), but takes account of social and sporting obligations.